TRYIN'
TO
MAKE IT

Adapting to the Bahamas

John Bregenzer

UNIVERSITY
PRESS OF
AMERICA

Copyright © 1982 by
University Press of America,Inc.™
P.O. Box 19101, Washington, D.C. 20036

Printed in the United States of America

ISBN (Perfect): 0-8191-2622-5
ISBN (Cloth): 0-8191-2621-7

Library of Congress Number: 82-45003

A project of this type requires much support
other than financial and intellectual.
This work is dedicated to all who waited for it.

ACKNOWLEDGMENTS

To the people and government of Eleuthera and the Bahamas go my deep thanks, friendship, and hope that somehow through this work and in other ways they will be repaid.

Indispensible financial support for this project was provided by the Research Council of the University of Dayton through a University grant for fieldwork in the summer of 1969 and through a National Science Foundation Institutional Grant for the summer of 1970. A grant from GAC Eleuthera Ltd. for an archaeological survey in the summer of 1972 allowed further ethnological work to be conducted following that project.

Although the entire Anthropology Department at the University of Minnesota has had a profound positive influence on me, three individuals must be singled out for special thanks. Long-time friend and fellow graduate student, Michael C. Robbins suggested this study in 1968 and has been a continual source of helpful guidance. Pertti J. Pelto was my advisor in the early years of my training, Luther P. Gerlach was my advisor in the later years. What merit I may show is to a large degree a result of the selfless and inspired efforts of my advisors.

Darryl Pickering, Michael Cronin, Gottfried Hodge, James Viehdeffer, and Robert Rusbosin performed like professionals in their fieldwork for me on Eleuthera.

Sandy Crabill and Sharon Nee graciously relieved pressures on me by adding to their own in typing this.

TABLE OF CONTENTS

CHAPTER 1

MYTH OF THE TROPICAL ISLE

> There's an island untarnished by
> time just 15 air minutes from Nassau,
> 50 air minutes from Miami via Pan Am.
> An island with no boardwalks, no
> drive-ins, no billboards, no neon, no
> garish trappings of tinsel "civiliza-
> tion."
> But it is an island of plenty.
> An island embraced by pink sand and
> turquoise sea. With green fields you
> can walk through and fill your arms
> with flowers. With age-old caves
> waiting to be discovered. With beaches
> that seem to run beyond the horizon . . .
> (Advertisement for Cape Eleuthera).

The object of this study is to set forth, docu-
ment, and explore the implications of an idea concerning the nature of human adaptation to a minor island of
the Caribbean. The idea is that the island is not
"insular," i.e. it is not isolated and insulated from
the forces that reverberate through the wider world,
not ecologically pristine and a place of natural abun-
dance, not for the natives a place of a tranquil and
easy life. Life on the island is and always has been
shaped by and utterly dependent on the outside world.
Not "insular," the island is "exposed."

This central generalization results from question-
ing what might be called "the myth of the tropical
isle." This myth does not seem to be held by people
who dwell on tropical islands, but by Westerners. The
ancient Greeks invested islands with a special aura in
their legends of Atlantis and in the fantastic island-
hopping voyages recited by Homer. The myth appears to
have developed with the development of European colonialism. Major representations of it appear in the paint-
ings of Gauguin and others influenced by him, and in
the writings of Defoe, Rousseau, Stevenson and Melville
(Smith 1960). In this century it is represented in
movies and on television, but the chief current pur-
veyor of the myth in a form least tempered by reality
is the tourist industry.

The essence of the myth is that tropical islands are a sort of Eden. Atlantis was conceived as the source of civilization when civilization was regarded as an unmixed blessing. With the coming of industrialism, linked to world exploration and colonialism, negative aspects of civilization came to be perceived and tropical islands came to be viewed as places free of these evils. They came to be regarded as places with abundant food provided free-for-the-taking by nature and therefore with little effort required to live a simple, uncomplicated life. Islands did not have the problems of the urban ratrace, crime, pollution, or any other evil associated with the industrial system, because they were supposedly isolated from that system.

"Insular" has come to mean "isolated." The association of "island" with isolation and abundant subsistence is so strong in the English language that a person consulting Roget's Thesaurus for a synonym of "isolated" will find: "isolation, insulation, insular; oasis, island" (1946 and reprintings: 26).

Eleuthera is the name of the island dealt with in this study. Technically it is not a tropical island since it is located about 100 miles north of the Tropic of Cancer, about 250 miles due east of southernmost Florida. The entire group of islands to which Eleuthera belongs, the Bahamas, is often ignored in discussions of the Caribbean. It is ignored because it is on the geographic margin of the Caribbean and has always been small in total population. In this study, Eleuthera will be considered tropical because it is widely perceived as such. It will be considered part of the Caribbean because, although small and peripheral, it has much in common with other Caribbean islands. Eleuthera is here considered to be a tropical island, part of the Caribbean, but not "insular," not in reality what the "myth of the tropical isle" posits it to be.

The purpose of this study is not to debunk the myth. Anyone who has objectively considered the conditions of life on tropical islands realizes that they fall short of an Eden defined as the antithesis of the evils of the industrial system. A lengthy study is not required to make this point. Further, myths can be regarded as socially approved psychological projections, or visions. If recognized as such and not confused with the actual, objective situation, myths can serve to

2

guide goal-directed behavior. A vision of life without
the evils of industrialism is a vital first step toward
emancipation from those evils.

The purpose of this study fits well with a recent
statement of the special purpose of anthropology within
the social sciences: "Anthropology focuses upon the
details of individual behavior in the context of situation and group. From the examination of such data,
statements can be made about the types of persisting
social structures as explanatory of the expected behavior of individuals in varying situations . . . . Its
abstractions arise from the empirical procedures of
natural science and its conclusions are subject to continuous testing through additional evidence" (Kimball
1975:366).

The purpose here is to present a generalization
regarding the island of Eleuthera: the place is exposed,
not isolated. It is subject to, shaped by, and adapted
to great and fluctuating forces from outside. This
generalization seems to illuminate many otherwise diverse
details of the situation there and even "explain expected behavior of individuals in varying situations."

If this study can be regarded as conventional in
presenting a generalization purporting to explain the
way of life of a group of people, it is not so conventional in the type of generalization presented. Anthropology has generated a long list of ethnographies that
view individual societies as islands, isolated from
other societies. Traits within the society are ex-
plained by indicating their functional relationship to
other traits within the same society. Seemingly exotic
or disfunctional traits "make sense" when viewed in the
cultural context of that society. This traditional
approach could be labeled the "closed system" approach.

This study takes what might be called the "open
system" approach. The way of life on Eleuthera is regarded as a system, but as a system which is a func-
tioning part in a much broader system. Traits are still
examined in relation to context, but a much broader view
of context is entertained. With exposure as a leitmo-
tiv, attention is constantly focused on context beyond
the here and now of Eleuthera.

Following this introductory chapter, the ecology
of the island is considered. The natural environment

3

is the most basic context for any human group. Different groups can adapt in diverging ways to the same environment, but a given environment constrains any group and at the same time offers opportunities for human exploitation unavailable in other environments. The ecological facts indicate that tropical islands in general and Eleuthera in particular were not "Gardens of Eden" in their pristine state and that they are at present far from their pristine state.

Chapter three establishes that the people of the island are not noble savages. This brief chapter is intended to give the reader some feeling for the complex reality of the Eleutheran people.

Chapter four examines the history of Eleuthera and the Bahamas in considerable detail. In the strategy of this study history is viewed as a crucial context for understanding the present. According to this view, the characteristics of the present human system on the island are the result of selection over time of practices that proved viable in coping with the particular situation of the Bahamas. Cycles of boom and bust caused by powerful forces in the wider world over which Bahamians have had little control characterize Bahamian history. Chapter three shows how the Eleutheran cultural situation developed to cope with these conditions.

Chapters five through eight are devoted to detailed discussion of the present cultural system of Eleuthera. Chapter five presents and discusses demographic statistics, derived mainly from the most recent census. This distant and detached perspective reveals some broader aspects of the culture that are poorly comprehended when one is immersed in the details of data derived from participant observation. Statistics on marital status give insight into the nature of the fundamental social unit, the family, on this island. Consideration of an age-sex pyramid of the population leads to the conclusion that a major solution to the problems of living on this exposed island is migration, particularly out-migration at about age sixteen for both males and females.

If the demographic chapter could be regarded as applying calipers to the outside of the Eleutheran system, the next, chapter six, "The Human System," looks inside the system to see how it works, to see how individuals and groups, statuses and roles articulate with each other. In any system, what happens in one part of

4

the system affects what happens in other parts. Consideration of the Eleutheran system shows considerable social fragmentation, a design feature that minimizes one part affecting other parts. Attention is given to how this characteristic developed in the system and why it persists.

Chapter seven, "Outward Appearances," is devoted to a verbal description of the Eleutheran system in operation. Any time a person observes a family, a business, a town, a city, he is viewing a human system in operation. With the preceding chapters as important background, a verbal tour of the South Administrative District of Eleuthera is taken in this chapter. The tour visits three "settlements" (what would be called "towns" in the United States). The three settlements are clearly ranked according to the amount of their involvement in the modern world. Rock Sound with a population of about 1,000, is the most involved, with virtually all adults engaged in wage labor related in some fashion to the tourist industry. Bannerman Town, with a population of about 100 is the other extreme. Here there is very little wage labor and most people are occupied with subsistence farming. The third settlement, Greencastle, is midway in population, 500, and midway in exposure. Here there are about equal numbers of farmers and wage laborers. Chapter seven specifies the range of variation of human communities on the island.

Chapter eight could be regarded as the "climax" of this study. Its title, "Inward Appearances," requires some explanation. The concern in this chapter is to determine whether, and if so how, individuals vary in their attitudes and values as the settlements vary in the amount of their involvement with the modern world. A fundamental postulate in many current social-scientific quarters is that there is such a thing as a "modern person" who differs in attitudes and values from a "traditional person." Persons taking this point of view generally feel that the way for developing nations, like the Bahamas, to develop to a state of modernity is for people to change their attitudes and values. Chapter eight presents the results of measuring attitudes and values in each of the three settlements described in chapter seven. The results indicate that there is no important difference in people between "traditional" Bannerman Town and "modern" Rock Sound. Greencastle, expected to be midway between the other two in any variation is found, in general, to have a more traditional

5

"inward appearance" than the settlement that is outwardly most traditional. Since many studies have shown that individuals do vary in attitudes and values with varying exposure to modern conditions, Eleuthera appears to be an exception. Discussion of this finding attempts to make Eleuthera not the exception which proves the rule, but perhaps the exception which improves the rule.

Chapters one through four provide background to a discussion of the current human system on Eleuthera. Chapters five through eight discuss the current system with an increasingly narrowing focus, leading in chapter eight to some possible lessons for humanity to be gained from the Eleutheran experience. The final chapter summarizes the view of Eleuthera as an exposed island and the part that this small subsystem plays in the total human system.

CHAPTER 2

ECOLOGY

We have evidence that the barren
island of Ascension aboriginally possessed less than half-a-dozen flower-
ing plants; yet many species have now
become naturalized on it, as they have
in New Zealand and on every other oceanic island which can be named. In
St. Helena there is every reason to
believe that the naturalized plants
and animals have nearly or quite ex-
terminated many native productions.
He who admits to the doctrine of the
creation of each separate species,
will have to admit that a sufficient
number of the best adapted plants and
animals were not created for oceanic
islands; for man has unintentionally
stocked them far more fully than did
nature (Darwin 1859:305).

Fifty miles east of Palm Beach, Florida is an
island called Grand Bahama. Five hundred ninety miles
southeast of this point is an island, near Haiti and
Cuba, known as Great Inagua. These are extremes of an
archipelago known as the Bahama Islands. Seldom rising
more than 200 feet above the sea and usually less than
50 feet in elevation are twenty-nine pieces of land
large enough to be considered islands. Interspersed
between the islands, the usually shallow and turquoise
unpolluted sea is dotted with 661 smaller pieces of
land called "cays" and thousands of individual rocks.

No rock other than limestone is to be found in the
composition of the Bahamas. Where borings have been
made, the bed of limestone has been found to be thousands of feet thick, similar to southern Florida and
the Yucatan. Unlike the peninsular areas, the Bahama
Islands appear to be built on a submarine mountain
range, exposed as volcanic rock in islands further south
in the Caribbean. The limestone was laid down by corals
beginning during the tertiary geologic period and continues today, as witnessed by the fact that the area
contains all three major types of reef: fringing, bar-
rier and atoll. The Bahama Islands have thus been
built over a period of perhaps 65,000,000 years as the

7

solidified remains of marine life were pushed upward by subterranean forces and shaped by the action of currents, waves, wind and rain.

When they had risen sufficiently above the sea to achieve the necessary independence from it, land plants and to a lesser extent land animals began to exist on these islands. Eventually there were myriad species occupying a range of habitats which could be classified crudely as coast versus interior, with the coastal areas importantly different on the sandy windward side from the rocky leeward side and the whole island importantly differing in habitat with differences in elevation.

From whence came these first plant and animal inhabitants of the Bahamas who were over time to establish a balanced if, compared to continents, thin and precarious ecosystem? It is important to realize that although the Bahamas are millions of years old, by the time they were formed, the continents were teeming with living things up to the level of mammals. The familiar story of Darwin's finches is important to understanding the special ecology of oceanic islands (those formed in the sea, as opposed to islands which are detached parts of continents). In the Galapogos Islands, Darwin found a number of closely related species of finch with different beaks and feeding habits: beaks for eating seeds, woodpecker-like beaks to feed on insect larvae under bark or in wood, parrot-like beaks for fruit and buds, and beaks adapted to feeding on free-flying insects. Darwin's explanation for this situation was that only a few numbers of one species of finch and no other birds from the South American continent had managed the long voyage to these islands. The descendents of these immigrants had maximized the use of available food and thereby increased their numbers by evolving into the witnessed specialized species. It is now generally recognized that what Darwin observed with finches applies as a general rule with plants and animals on oceanic islands:

> Man has imported to Hawaii every important source of food grown on the land, as he has to a vast number of islands the world over . . . .(Aboriginally) the islands have been populated by a few groups of plants and animals that fortuitously have passed through the seive of difficulty of

8

MAP 1: THE BAHAMA ISLANDS

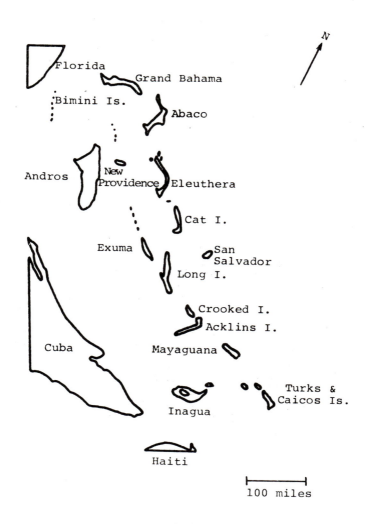

overseas transport, reached the islands, and surmounted the mostly overwhelming hazards of survival and colonization . . . . The flora and fauna
are disharmonic, or unbalanced, as compared to the continents. Many major
taxonomic categories of organisms never
reached the islands. Only a few ancestral immigrants gave rise to the entire
endemic biota. Thus, it has been estimated that the endemic flora of about
2,000 higher plants has arisen from
about 275 ancestral immigrant stocks,
and about the same number gave rise to
the 5,000 or more Hawaiian insects.
This means that possibly only one successful plant or insect colonization
has occurred every 20,000 or 30,000
years . . . .(Zimmerman 1963:58-59).

Prior to the coming of people, the ecology of islands is different from that of continents. Since the
native biota is the result of adaptive radiation of only
a few strains, it might be suspected that it is precarious, that the introduction of other strains by humans
could result in almost total, certainly "revolutionary",
change in the ecosystem. That this is indeed the case
is indicated in the conclusion to a thorough study of
the ecological history of the outer Leeward Islands
(Antigua, Barbuda, and Anguilla):

In the ecology of the outer Lee-
wards, as of other oceanic islands,
the dynamic relationship that exists
between man and the organic environment
he exploits is illuminated with excep-
tional clarity. Lacking ecological resistance, which increases with the com-
plexity of plant and animal communities,
the islands are highly vulnerable both
to the destruction of their native flora
and fauna and to the invasion of alien
species. First among the aliens is man
himself. Ecologically dominant throughout, he has transformed the soils, vegitation, and animal life of the islands
from the beginnings of aboriginal occupation (Harris 1964:142).

10

Few land animals are found natively on oceanic islands. In the Bahamas it appears that only lizards and
some nonpoisonous snakes established themselves aboriginally. In the early days of European settlement most
of the islands of the Bahamas were home to a large, edi-
ble iguana reported to resemble chicken in taste. Human
predation has extinguished this creature everywhere
except in the protected Exuma Cays Land and Sea Park.
Birds are more plentiful than land animals on islands.
In the Bahamas flamingos, being tasty, suffered a fate
similar to the iguana and are found now only in protected circumstances, especially on Great Inagua Island
(Hannau 1970:71, 105). Most of the rest of the forty-
four endemic species of birds reported by Riley (1905)
survive widely in the Bahamas. Many other species migrate through these islands.

It is in the vegetation of the Bahamas that the
really drastic changes have occurred. European settlers
found only one native plant of any substantial commercial value, braziletto wood, which was used as a dye.
The supply was quickly exhausted. What little remains
today is used only to brew a native tea. A few other
native plants are used as curatives in Bahamian folk
medicine, but the majority of plants used this way are
alien to the native flora of the Bahamas (Higgs 1969).
Agriculture based on alien plants was essential for
human existence in the Bahamas and it is agriculture
that produced revolutionary changes in the natural ecology of these islands. From present agricultural practices it is apparent that both the system used and the
basic list of crops derive from the original settlers
of the Caribbean, Arawak and Carib Indian groups. These
peoples built permanent settlements near the shore and
subsisted by fishing and growing crops by a method vari-
ously known as shifting cultivation, swidden agriculture,
and slash-and-burn agriculture.

Examination of the map of Eleuthera shows that
settlements are now spaced roughly ten miles apart,
almost always on the leeward shore, but in any event
protected from the winds and waves of the Atlantic.
The pattern is particularly striking here because this
is a lineal island, 100 miles long and an average of
two miles in width. In a famous paper, Robert L.
Carniero has carefully examined the implications of
slash-and-burn agriculture for settlement patterns.
Carniero finds that where walking is not difficult, as
is the case on most Caribbean islands, people will walk

11

a maximum of five miles to their fields (1960:232). It would be difficult to find a more reasonable explanation for the actual geographic positioning of settlements on Eleuthera.

In the Eleutheran and Carribean variant of shifting agriculture, only small areas, seldom exceeding two acres, are cleared by the farmer, almost always working alone. A variety of crops are planted in each field, placed wherever there are pockets of soil in eroded depressions of the limestone; the largest, most fertile such depressions being used for fruit trees. A field is generally used only one year, then left a number of years in fallow. At the turn of the century the fallow period was estimated to be 15-20 years (Mooney 1905:174). Current observations indicate that fields are still in a state of dense undergrowth when cleared. This implies that the fallow period is as long as possible, but not as long as farmers would desire for ease of clearing and certainly not nearly long enough for the lands to achieve any semblance of a "natural" ecological state. A further implication of the short fallow period is that all land on which agriculture is possible (and Eleutherans are wizards at making seemingly infertile land bear good crops) has been cleared and used repeatedly for the cultivation of plants alien to the native vegitation of the island. One must conclude that the present vegetation of Eleuthera bears very little resemblance to the natural state of the island.

Sapodilla, soursop, pigeon pea, pawpaw, mamey, mango, manioc, guava, Guinea corn, hog plum; these are words which will whet the appetite of a hungry Bahamian or anyone who enjoys Bahamian food. None are part of the natural vegetation of either the Bahamas or the Caribbean. They are selected from a list of alien plants found on Antigua (Harris 1965:54-57). According to Harris, the majority of alien plants found in the Caribbean were brought there by the original settlers, the Arawak and Carib, but it is a small majority because the colonial period brought considerable additions from Asia, Europe and Africa.

This brief consideration of island ecology indicates that it is a mistake to view tropical eceanic islands as Gardens of Eden. It would seem closer to the truth to view them as moonlike. To be suitable for human habitation considerable life-support baggage must accompany any settlers. Abundant food and an easy life

MAP 2: ELEUTHERA

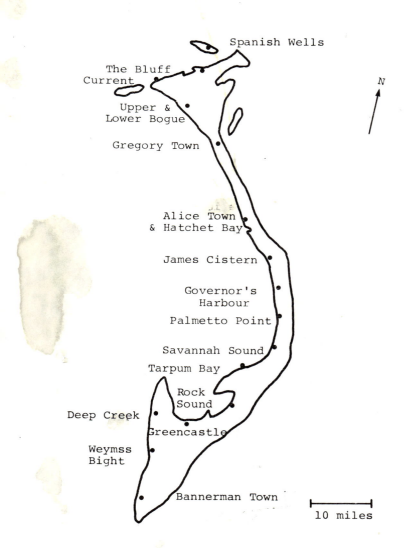

Spanish Wells

The Bluff
Current

Upper &
Lower Bogue

Gregory Town

Alice Town
& Hatchet Bay

James Cistern

Governor's
Harbour

Palmetto Point

Savannah Sound

Tarpum Bay

Rock
Sound

Deep Creek

Greencastle

Weymss
Bight

Bannerman Town

N

⊢━━━━━━━┥
10 miles

is available for some in the tropical island outposts
of human settlement, but it is a sobering fact that in
1972 local production accounted for only 15.1% of the
$62.7 million food bill of the Bahama Islands (Dupuch
1974:145).

CHAPTER 3

ISLANDERS

U.S. Tourist: You speak a form of broken English
around here, don't you?
Eleutheran: Yes sir, and so do you.

What are the people of Eleuthera like? The question seems very simple, but it is difficult to answer.
The answer is difficult because different observers will give answers that vary with differences in their prior experience and differences in the interest of their attention. Answers to such a question inevitably say something about the observer as well as the observed.
The answer given here is brief and unapologetically impressionistic and anecdotal. Following chapters present a good deal of factual detail about the people.
This chapter is intended merely to sketch in broad outline a notion of the complex, living reality of the islanders of Eleuthera as seen by the author.

First it is necessary, and easy, to correct the mythical view of the islander as a carefree noble savage. A few Eleutherans do indeed spend their days indolently in the shade of a tree. It is not a palm tree on the beach, but a large Guinep tree in an area of Rock Sound seldom traversed by tourists. The people here are not happy. They maintain that the cares of life are responsible for their unhappy condition. Fellow Eleutherans stigmatize them as incorrigible alcoholics, referring to them collectively as "The Assembly of Rum," a parody of the local church "The Assembly of God," or individually as "Moonglow Men," in reference to the fact that about the only work they do is occasionally stevedoring mailboats, such as the "Moonglow." Thankfully they are few, only about a dozen among the 1,000 people of Rock Sound, and this is the only settlement on Eleuthera that has an island equivalent of skid row.

The Eleutheran is much more like the U.S. American than like the noble savage. Not only the language, but the way of life of both these peoples are forms of "broken English." Eleuthera and the U.S. colonies were both founded by the English about three centuries ago. Present differences between the two are more differences of emphasis than basic differences in kind. This basic similarity makes Eleuthera a good test case for studying the influences of an island environment on culture.

15

Eleuthera can be regarded as a well-controlled natural experiment in which, by contrast with the mainland culture of the U.S., the effects of the island environment on English culture can be observed.

Not all the differences in culture are due directly to the island environment. The outsider's first observation is likely to be that most of the people are black. Many U.S. tourists return from the Bahamas believing that Bahamians are bilingual, capable of speaking both British English and some exotic African tongue. In fact Bahamians, like many U.S. blacks, are bidialectical. The dialect used with tourists is no more identical to British English than the "Elizabethan English" supposedly spoken by some isolated Appalacians. The vernacular has a few features that are unique to the Bahamas, but it is essentially identical to Black English as spoken in the United States (Dillard 1972).

Besides language, many other aspects of Eleutheran culture are more "Afro-American" than "island." Eleutheran jukeboxes contain some music recorded by Bahamians, but the large majority of selections are U.S. produced "soul" music. Like other Afro-Americans, Eleutherans value verbal skill and verbosity. A quiet person is suspect and one who can speak at great length is esteemed (Abrahams 1964, Kochman 1969). Eleutherans share the Afro-American love of clothing. Special occasions, especially weddings and national holidays, will find them outfitted in the latest U.S. fashions.

The second observation of the outsider regarding Eleutherans is likely to be that they are very religious. References to God and the Bible are heavily interspersed in the flow of conversation. To the statement, "I'll see you later," is likely to come the response, "If God spare life." Younger Eleutherans are less overtly religious, but their convictions seem to be strong. In a conversation with a young construction worker, the author was asked whether he thought Americans would actually set foot on the moon. To an affirmative reply came the response: "The day they do that, that's the day I'm going to repent."

High religiosity may be regarded more as a feature of Afro-American culture (Herskovits 1941) than as a result of the island environment. However, the form Eleutheran religiosity takes evidences an Eleutheran trait that is a major concern in this study, and which

16

does seem to be directly related to the exposed nature of the island environment. In religion and in many other ways, Eleutherans appear to be individually autonomous and not socially cohesive.

To spend Sunday in an Eleutheran settlement is an unusual experience for someone from the contemporary U.S. Except to go to church and return, virtually nobody leaves home. Since tourists do not stay in the settlements but in resort enclaves, businesses are not open. The first Sunday the author and his students spent on the island, it was only Eleutheran Christian charity that enabled them to obtain something to eat.

Church congregations are certainly cohesive social units, but the small settlements are divided into a surprising number of congregations, seven in a settlement of 1,000, three in a settlement of only 100. As in the U.S., people feel that their particular brand of Christianity is better than other brands.

A striking example of religious individualism and evidence of respect for it among Eleutherans is the case of the man in one of the settlements who purchased an amplified loudspeaker and who sermonizes nightly to his seemingly indifferent neighborhood from his front porch. Although nobody else engages in this particular activity, it exemplifies how Eleutheran individualism contrasts with other forms individualism might take. Eleutheran individualism consists of a high respect for the rights and personal freedom of others. It is more imposed on the individual than sought. It necessarily implies low social cohesiveness.

One last characteristic must be mentioned in any discussion of what Eleutherans are like. Eleutherans are poor. They have substantially less money than the tourists who flock to their island, thus they are fully aware of being poor. The vast majority do not succumb to despair in this situation. They manage as best they can. A poignant example of an Eleutheran coping with poverty is the now fairly successful man who confided that he went for years without underwear in order to feed his family. During this time, he worried about getting a rip in his pants, not so much because of exposing himself, but because people would realize that he could not afford underwear.

Eleuthera illustrates that being poor and knowing

it may be necessary conditions for "the culture of poverty", as found in the slums of San Juan, Mexico City, and U.S. urban areas, but not sufficient conditions. Eleutherans have not given up. To the question, "How are you doing?", Eleutherans will generally reply with the stock phrase, "Tryin' to make it."

CHAPTER 4

HISTORY

Some say one mountain did sink in de sea
An' leave all 'ee peaks jookin' out;
Columbus soon come wid dem sailin'
    boats tree,
An' spy dem lil isles ta de sout'
        (Wallace 1970:13)

Well before the arrival of Columbus, the Bahamas
had been discovered and settled. Although the prehistory of the Caribbean is yet but poorly known, and
best known from the larger islands (Rouse 1964, 1966
and references), sixteen possible village sites have
been located in the Bahamas (Granberry 1973:27). None
of the village sites has been systematically excavated,
but there has been considerable site-survey work, test
excavation, and excavation of sites other than villages.
The literature on Bahamian prehistory has been surveyed
by Granberry (1955) and Hoffman (1967). Information
continues to accumulate. In the summer of 1972, two
aboriginal middens were recorded in the Cape Eleuthera
development zone of South Eleuthera. Native Americans
clearly visited Eleuthera to harvest what is still a
major food resource, a large sea-snail known as the
conch. There is as yet no information to indicate that
there were any permanent settlements on Eleuthera by
these people.

It is now generally accepted that Columbus' landfall in the New World on October 12, 1492 was San Salvador Island in the Bahamas (Wolper 1964). There he
encountered people who called themselves "Lukku-caire,"
or "Island People," subsequently rendered "Lucayans."
Although the first human settlement of Caribbean islands
may have been as early as 5,000 B.C. (Cruxent and Rouse
1969), there is no reason to believe that the Bahamas
were settled before about 750 A.D. The Lucayans and
their predecessors appear as part of the Arawak invasion
of the Caribbean which began from South America at about
the time of Christ. Their settlement of the Bahamas
appears to coincide with their displacement by the mar-
auding Carib peoples (Cruxent and Rouse 1969, Hoffman
1970).

On his first voyage Columbus captured a few of
these people that he misnamed "Indians" and brought

them back to Spain. In 1498 on his third voyage, he
shipped back 600. Prior to this massive shipment,
forced peonage and tribute were introduced in the new
Spanish colonies. The peoples of the Caribbean were
enslaved early and vigorously, but it was an unsuccess-
ful enterprise. How rapidly the natives perished under
the new conditions is attested by conservative estimates
of the population of Hispaniola. In 1492, the population was between 200,000 and 300,000. By 1508 it was
down to 60,000. 1514 showed 14,000 and 1548 less than
500 (Williams 1970:33).

Although details are sparce, it is certain that the
archipelago extending from north of Hispaniola and north-
east of Cuba toward Florida that came to be known as the
Bahamas (Sp. bahamar, "shallow"), was depopulated very
early. An early chronicler wrote: "Within the twenty
years that have elapsed since the Spaniards arrived
there they claim to have explored 406 of these islands
(to the north of Cuba) and to have carried off 40,000
inhabitants of both sexes as slaves, to satisfy their
unquenchable appetite for gold" (Martyr 1511). Later
scholars think that 40,000 is probably an exaggerated
estimate of the total aboriginal population of the
Bahamas and would add that Lucayans served not only in
goldmines, but on plantations and especially as divers
in the pearl fisheries of Margarita, near Trinidad: "By
this fishing trade the Spaniards have destroyed all the
people of the Lucay Islands . . . they were marvelously
dexterous at swimming and diving"(Las Casas 1560). Most
of the capturing of Lucayans seems to have occurred
between 1509 and 1512. During that brief period, the
price per head went from five to 150 gold pesos. According to Sauer, the "discovery" of Florida by Ponce de
Leon in 1513 was in fact an extension beyond the empty
islands of slave hunting (1966:160).

The Bahamas remained empty for almost a century and
a half. The Spanish found no use for them and were wary
of even sailing through them because of the dangerous
shallow waters. Despite this wariness, an entire fleet
of seventeen Spanish ships wrecked off the island of
Abaco in 1595. In 1625 there was a French attempt to
settle Abaco, but that colony lasted less than a year
(Bellin 1725).

English interest in the Caribbean can be said to
have begun in 1527, when John Rut sailed to Puerto Rico
and Hispaniola to trade with the Spanish colonists.

In the second half of the sixteenth century, the Afro-Americanization of the Caribbean began in earnest with the slave trading of Englishman John Hawkins. During this same period, English and French pirates became a serious threat to the Spanish, often lurking in the treacherous waters of the Bahamas.

In 1629 Charles I of England laid claim to the Bahamas by deeding them, along with Carolina, to Sir Robert Heath. Heath never established his intended Bahamian colony. In 1633 the French claimed five of the islands and likewise failed to colonize them. The first permanent European colony in the Bahamas was established on the island of Eleuthera in the winter of 1647-48. These were times of English religious-political strife between Anglican Royalists or "loyalists" and Puritan Republicans or "independents." In 1620 English Puritans had founded a colony at Plymouth, Massachusetts. In 1647 William Sayle, a Puritan who had served two terms as governor or Bermuda, sought funds in London to establish another such colony. It was to be located on "Eleutheria and the Bahama Islands." Sayle derived the word "Eleutheria" from the Greek "eleuthros," meaning "freedom." He specified freedom in his colony to mean that there would be republicanism, a single legislature and religious toleration, but not the abolition of rights of property or privilege.

An investment of L100 made on an "Eleutherian Adventurer." Few of these adventurers emigrated to the Bahamas. They were shareholders in a commercial venture and it is doubtful that any recouped their investment. Sayle's scheme raised enough money to finance the voyage of seventy colonists, mostly from Bermuda, in two ships. There is little consensus or data concerning the location on the island of this first settlement. Young favors the northern part of the island and Craton the center (Young 1966, Craton 1968).

Two freedoms the colonists did not find on the island were freedom from strife and freedom from physical want. Shortly after arrival the group broke into two factions, one headed by Sayle and the other by Captain Butler. Sayle left with a majority of the group and both ships to settle elsewhere on the island. Near the harbor of the second settlement the larger ship "struck and was cast away" (Lefroy 1879). One life and all the provisions were lost. Sayle took the remaining ship and eight men to Virginia to seek aid. There they received supplies and the loan of a large (twenty-five ton) ship. In April of 1650 a larger amount of supplies was received from two Puritan churches in Boston. The Bostonians stayed a month on the island when they delivered the supplies, earning themselves the distinction of being the first tourists to the island. Sayle and company treated them well. To repay the relief expedition they loaded ten tons of Braziletto dyewood for the return voyage. This was to be sold to pay the costs of the expedition and any remaining funds were to be donated to a new college in Boston. Remaining funds amounted to L124, the third largest sum donated at that point to Harvard.

The colony was augmented during its first years by a number of banished Bermudians. Political dissidents, freed slaves, and a number of troublesome and unproductive slaves found themselves making the one-way southwesterly voyage (Wilkinson 1933). During these years the main sources of income appear to have been Braziletto wood, which sold for L12 per ton, and ambergris, which sold for L4 per ounce, but supplies of both were limited and declining. A Spanish treasure ship cast ashore on Abaco in July 1657, netting L2,600, but this sort of windfall was undependable and probably offset by periodic Spanish and French raids on the colonists. It should be noted at this point that a pattern of life was being established that required movement from place to place to garner money and that people tended not to specialize in any one money-making activity, but derived their income from multiple sources. As will be seen in this and following chapters, migration and occupational multiplicity are important distinguishing characteristics of the Bahamian way of life to the present day.

The little colony did not prosper, but it grew. The early growth of the Bahamas seems to be associated with overcrowding on Bermuda and the increasing English migration during these times to the American colonies. In 1666 the island of New Providence, fifty miles west of Eleuthera, was settled from Bermuda. Within five years that island exceeded Eleuthera in population and its settlement, Nassau, was recognized as the capital of the Bahamas. The first census of the Bahamas in 1671 shows that New Providence had 913 residents, consisting of 257 males, 243 females and 413 slaves in 127 households. Eleuthera at that time had only 184 residents, 77 males, 77 females and 30 slaves. Since trade was centered in Nassau, Eleuthera's link to the

outside world was found there. Eleuthera had quickly
become an "out-island," its economically similar settlements having more important ties with the capital than
with each other. When other islands of the archipelago
were settled, they also became "out-islands". The rela-
tionships between the islands came to resemble a great
wheel with "spokes" extending to the "hub" of Nassau,
New Providence.

The first period of Bahamian prosperity, like all
such periods to follow, arrived and left fortuitously,
not the result of any internal development of the Bahamian culture, but of changing conditions in the wider
world, over which Bahamians had no control. For the
period from 1691 to 1717 Nassau became the world capital
of piracy. Although the waters of the Bahamas were
treacherous to the unknowledgeable, and therefore provided a good lurking place for pirates, other places in
the Caribbean proved more convenient prior to 1691.
Chief among these places were the island of Tortuga,
off the northern coast of Hispaniola, the island of
Providence, off Nicaragua, and Port Royal, opposite
Kingston, Jamaica. By 1641 the Spaniards were able to
drive the pirates from Providence.

Jamaica became increasingly incensed as the pirates
became decreasingly scrupulous over their prey, and drove
them out by 1685. At this time some pirates established
themselves in the southern Bahamas, not far from Tortuga,
and encountered no resistance from the small, weak government of the Bahamas. Tortuga, the pirate stronghold,
was under the control of France. When the Anglo-French
conflict, later known as the Seven Years War, reached
the Caribbean in 1691, the last of the English pirates
left Tortuga and established themselves without resis-
tence in the capital of the Bahamas.

Various estimates place the number of pirates in
Nassau during these years at about 1,000. Included
were all the famous names of English piracy: the "lady"
pirates Mary Read and Anne Bonney who sailed with "Calico
Jack" Rackham and Stede Bonnet, Charles Vane, and Edward
Teach, alias "Blackbeard," to name but a few. Attacking
not only Spanish and French vessels, but anything in
sight, the pirates generated British opposition that
quickly overcame them. Letters of complaint from citizens, captains, and the governors of every British
maritime colony descended on King George I. Astutely,
the King sent reformed pirate and inveterate slaver

Woodes Rodgers to end the complaints. Rodgers arrived in 1718, accompanied by four warships, to assume governorship of the Bahamas and declare amnesty for all pirates who reformed. Overwhelmed by force, the pirates accepted the amnesty. Although many reverted briefly to their previous ways, most left the Bahamas and the age of piracy was over.

Returning to England in 1721, Rodgers was rewarded by George I by being given the Great Seal of the Bahamas emblazoned: EXPULSIS PIRATIS RESTITUTA COMMERCIA. This remained the motto of the Bahamas until political independence in 1973. Only the first part of the motto had reality at the time. With the departure of the pirates the islands fell into an economic stupor. When Rodgers returned to serve a second term as governor from 1729 to 1732 he refused any salary because, "I found the place so very poor and thin of inhabitants." Total population of the colony in a census of 1731 was 925 free and 453 slaves (Craton 1968:116). 1737 seems to be the record low point of the economy. The Spanish prevented any salt raking in the southern Bahamas. No provisions were sent from the nearby mainland colonies. The governor reported to London that the people were forced to subsist only on crabs, fish, and wild fruit.

A form of commerce came to the Bahamas in 1739 when war was declared between England and Spain. Nassau became a base of legal privateering against Spanish ships and a link in the illicit trade from the British mainland colonies to the French colonies and from thence to the besieged Spanish colonies. Although this "War of Jenkin's Ear" lasted less than a year, the privateering and the illicit "Monte Christe" trade lasted until 1763, the end of the Seven Years War. In that year the Bahamian economy once more slipped into the doldrums.

In 1744, during this second period of Bahamian prosperity, a census was taken which shows Eleuthera to be clearly peripheral to Nassau in population. In that year the population of Nassau's New Providence Island was 2,063, the population of Eleuthera and small, adjacent Harbour Island was only 240 (Bruce 1782). With 200 square miles of land area to New Providence's 80, Eleuthera's function was to supply foodstuffs to Nassau. From this time until the census of 1901 the population growth of Eleuthera exceeded that of New Providence (Sharer 1955). In 1901 New Providence had a population of 12,534, Eleuthera 10,499. As time progressed

Eleuthera was clearly doing more than merely supplying foodstuffs to Nassau.

Before attempting to account for this 120 year period of population growth on Eleuthera, it is important to discuss three events occurring outside the Bahamas which had tremendous impact within the small colony: the successful revolt of the thirteen mainland colonies that resulted in the creation of the United States of America, the British Emancipation Act of 1833, and the United States Civil War.

While Bahamians were eking out an existence, relying for a large portion of their income on what can appropriately be called "penny-ante parasitic activities," the thirteen British mainland colonies were building a substantial economy based on large-scale plantation agriculture, manufacturing, and trade. "New England" seems an especially apt phrase because the mainland colonies were becoming a source of direct competition with the mother country (Williams 1970). What most concerns the Bahamas in the American Revolution is the non-revolutionaries, "Loyalists," located principally in the plantation-oriented southern colonies. Due to immigration of Loyalists and their slaves, the population of the Bahamas tripled in the five years between 1783 and 1788. The proportion of slaves in the population increased from less than half to three quarters (Craton 1968:162). It was at this time that most of the Bahamian out-islands were settled. New Providence surged in population, but Eleuthera and Harbour Island apparently gained not at all (Wylly 1789), a fact which may be important in understanding why Eleutheran culture differs from that of other Bahamian Islands.

The principal crop of the newcomers was long-staple "sea island" cotton, an heirloom of the Arawak. Prosperity marked the first years of its recultivation, continuing a third period of general prosperity that had begun by preying on trade between the rebel States and the Caribbean. By the end of 1785, 2,476 acres of long staple cotton had been planted and 124 tons exported. In 1787, 4,500 acres were planted and 219 tons exported (Craton 168:170). If inflation is a gauge of a booming economy, in which demand exceeds supply, the Bahamas were booming. Food prices in Nassau doubled between 1784 and 1786. The increase in population and shortage of food produced lasting benefits for long-established, food-producing Eleuthera. Declining soil fertility and insects soon severely limited the amount of cotton that could be grown, but the population increment to the colony was not lost, even on the main cotton producing islands (Sharer 1955:83).

The most important thing that ever happened in the Bahamas, at least from the viewpoint of the black majority of the population, was emancipation. "August Monday," the first Monday of August, is to this day a most important Bahamian holiday, a time of solidarity in which many return to their homes in the out-islands. The Emancipation Act was designed to come into force August 1, 1843, but included a period of "apprenticeship," similar to indentured labor, which lasted four years. Slaves in England and her colonies became fully free on August 1, 1838.

Slavery in what must be called the "backwater colony" of the Bahamas took a form different from that of the more lucrative cotton and sugar producing colonies. During the brief period of Loyalist influence the situation was different, but by 1831 when the Bahamian human ecosystem had restabilized, the ratio of slaves to "free persons of color" is astoundingly low: three slaves to one free (Craton 1968:187). During the heyday of the sugar islands, the ratio ranged from twenty-one to one on Grenada to seventy-four to one on Barbados (Williams 1970:190).

Further insight into the atypicality of the Bahamas within the Afro-American system of slavery is available because the Emancipation Act called for records of compensation paid for slaves freed. Compensation was determined by the average economic value of the slaves to the particular economy. The value of total exports of each colony was divided by the number of slaves in the colony. This ratio was applied to the total compensation of L20,000,000 to determine the amount due each colony.

The low productivity of the Bahamas is reflected in the fact that the amount paid there per slave was the lowest of all the colonies, less than L13. This can be compared with L52 for British Guiana; L50 for Trinidad, and L20 for Jamaica, a colony which had almost half the slaves in the British Caribbean (Craton 1968:203).

It might be suspected that the amount paid per slave was low because the number of slaves per owner was high. The same records indicate that this is not true. In the Bahamas 1,418 claims were filed for 7,734 slaves; a ratio of five slaves per claim, the lowest of any colony. For the entire British West Indies 38,218 claims were filed for 540,559 slaves, an average of 14 slaves per claim (Williams 1970:283). The idea that large-scale slave plantations typified Caribbean islands proves to be a misconception.

It should be recognized that means and not modes have been presented. A few owners with a large number of slaves could mask the fact that the majority had less than average. Williams demonstrates that this was indeed the case in the British Caribbean, concluding that "the British West Indies were . . . producing for export with an economy geared to subsistence production" (1970:286). In the Bahamas eleven masters claimed more than 100 slaves, with one claiming 376 (Craton 1968:204). With perhaps two or three slaves, it would seem that the typical "plantation" in the Bahamas was a very small-time operation indeed.

One last fact from the records of emancipation is important to understanding the nature of Bahamian slavery. The percentage employed as domestic slaves, as opposed to field slaves, was twice that of any other colony. For the Bahamas the figure is thirty-two percent. For the entire British West Indies, the figure is thirteen percent. Again, Williams' assessment for the area holds doubly for the Bahamas: "It was more like a system of household management than a commercial plantation economy" (1970:285).

Like the Loyalist invasion, emancipation caused no fluctuation in the steady growth of Eleutheran population toward its 1901 zenith. Neither did the Bahamian repercussions of the United States Civil War.

The mid-nineteenth century saw the advent of the steamship. In 1851 the Bahamas passed an act to encourage steam navigation between New York and Nassau. The first tourist ship arrived that year, but burned in Nassau's harbor, discouraging the effort until 1859 when a contract was signed with Cunard for monthly New York-Nassau service. In 1860 the government began construction on the first hotel in the Bahamas, Nassau's still operating Royal Victoria. Civil War in the United States stopped the nascent tourist trade, but provided a far more lucrative source of income. Commerce was once more restored, this time by running the Northern blockade to bring supplies to the Southern states. Civil War period trade statistics in Table 3-1 show the tremendous impact of blockade-running on the Bahamian economy, the demise of the sailing ship, and the extreme brevity of this fourth period of prosperity.

Nassau was transformed during this period. Many individual fortunes were made. It was not unusual for a common sailor to receive $1,500. for a single trip. More significantly, for the first time, the government shared in the prosperity through duties levied on the goods. Government salaries were increased twenty-five percent, Bay Street was widened and provided with curbs and lights, the Bahamas Police Force was created, the Royal Victoria Hotel was quickly completed and the public debt was wiped out.

But the bubble soon burst. By 1869 the credit of the government was seriously threatened, government salaries were three months in arrears, the new hotel was put up for sale with not a single offer to buy it, and the 34 new street lamps were seldom lit.

This brief prosperity and sudden depression had little effect in the Out-Islands.   A recent historian on the Bahamas comments: "The Out-Islands suffered least, for they gained least from the brief war years. For them life went on like an endless and uneventful dream" (Craton 1968:238). The same historian regards the years 1865 to 1914 as the period of the "forgotten colony." It should be recalled that it was during this period that the Out-Island of Eleuthera came to rival New Providence in population. The colony may have been forgotten, but clearly something more than an "endless, uneventful dream" was happening on Eleuthera.

While successive waves of prosperity and depression washed over the conspicuous capital of the Bahamas, agricultural Eleuthera was slowly becoming the world center for the production of pineapples. The plant derives from the Carib aboriginies (Sauer 1966:57). Like so many other of the native American crops, the details of its introduction to the Bahamas are presently unknown, but in 1726 a Bahamian governor wrote that the pineapples of his islands were the best in America. Production centered on Eleuthera and nearby Cat Island because the soils there proved to be best suited to the plant. By the first decade of the nineteenth century, three varieties were being grown: English, Sugar Loaf and Spanish

TABLE 3-1: CIVIL WAR PERIOD TRADE STATISTICS

	Imports L's	Exports L's	Ships Arriving		Ships Departing	
			Sail	Steam	Sail	Steam
1860	234,029	157,350	-	-	-	-
1861	274,584	195,584	2	2	1	3
1862	1,250,322	1,007,755	74	32	109	46
1863	4,295,316	3,308,567	27	113	48	173
1864	5,346,112	4,672.398	6	105	2	165
1865	-	-	0	35	0	31

Scarlet. Up to 36,000 fruit to the acre were produced.
In 1802 a traveler noted that the fruit, technically a
swollen flower stem, while almost priceless in London
was selling for a dollar a hundred in Nassau (McKinnen
1804). By midcentury the Bahamas had become the world's
first large-scale producer of pineapples. Four years
after emancipation the first shipment was exported to
the United States. In 1857 a canning factory was opened
at Governor's Harbour in the Center of Eleuthera. When
the Bahamas issued its first postage stamp in 1859, the
design featured a pineapple. In 1864, the last year of
the Civil War, 229,226 dozen pineapples were exported.
In 1873 the figure was 381,222 dozen in addition to the
more than a million cans exported from Governor's Harbour. 1892 must be considered the peak year of the
pineapple boom. Almost 700,000 dozen pineapples were
exported. Further canneries had been opened at Rock
Sound, Eleuthera, Harbour Island, Abaco, and Nassau.
The "Sloop John B" of song fame is remembered on Eleuthera as one of the vessels engaged mainly in hauling
pineapples from Governor's Harbour to Nassau.

For more than a century Eleuthera slowly increased
in population and prosperity from the pineapple trade,
contrasting markedly with Nassau's roller-coaster economy. For a time it must have seemed to the inhabitants
that their economy was secure, not exposed like Nassau
to capricious world events. If so, this state of mind
was a delusion. An event of very minor importance in
world history extinguished Eleuthera's pineapple trade.
In 1894, Sanford B. Dole became the first president of

Hawaii. As part of Hawaii's annexation to the United States in 1898, a duty of seven dollars per thousand was placed on foreign pineapples. Florida increased production of pineapples, benefiting from rail service to the Eastern markets. Cuba and Jamaica increased production despite the tariff because they possessed ample sugar for canning and regular steamship service. These events were clearly unforeseen in the Bahamas. From 1892 to 1901 production increased tenfold, yielding export of 7,233,012 dozen in 1901, but prices had dropped ninety percent. Exports plummeted to 521,428 dozen in 1902 and by 1946 were down to only 20,000 (Craton 1968:247-249).

The crash of the pineapple trade initiated an exodus of population from Eleuthera of such an extent that the island has not yet recovered its 1901 population. Table 3-2, derived from twentieth-century censuses of the Bahamas, documents this fact and provides important background for a discussion of Eleuthera and the Bahamas in this century.

TABLE 3-2: TWENTIETH CENTURY POPULATION

Year	New Providence	Eleuthera*	Grand Bahama	Other Out-I	Total
1901	12,537	10,499	1,780	28,919	53,735
1911	13,554	8.119	1,824	32,447	55,944
1921	12,975	7,574	1,695	30,814	53.031
1931	19,756	7,527	2,241	30,304	59,828
1943	29,391	7,864	2,333	29,258	68,846
1953	46,125	7,596	4,095	27.025	84,841
1963	80,907	9,093	8,230	31,990	130,220
1970	101,503	9,468	25,859	31,982	168,812

*Includes Harbour Island and Spanish Wells

In the period from 1911 to 1921 the total population of the Bahama Islands declined. World War I seems to be responsible for this. Although only 670 Bahamians served in the British armed forces, with 50 dying, the Bahamas contributed L47,000 to the war effort, a sum large enough to produce severe strains in the small economy. The Bank of Nassau failed in 1916. Severe shortages of food and other supplies ensued. When the war concluded in 1918, many Bahamians had left the country. 2,500 had left the preceding July, hired to improve the port of Charleston, South Carolina.

Doubtless many never returned to the Bahamas. An additional survival tactic had been added to the Bahamian repertoire: work in the United States accompanied by either temporary of permanent migration.

During World War II substantial numbers of Bahamians contributed to U.S. agricultural production through an arrangement between the two governments known as "going on the contract." On the island of Andros, Otterbein found that two-thirds of the men in the settlement of Long Bay Cays had engaged in this work (1966:31). A similar situation is found on Eleuthera. It comes as quite a surprise to anyone holding a view of the Bahamas as isolated to encounter a subsistence farmer in a seemingly remote settlement who is intimately familiar with Oregon, or who has worked for the Green Giant Company in Minnesota. In the next chapter of this work evidence is presented that migration to the United States is at present an important, though usually overlooked, component of the Eleutheran and Bahamian survival system.

1920 to 1933 was another fortuitous boom period in the Bahamas. It was the era of prohibition in the United States and Bahamian bootlegging. During the period Nassau's population increased 52%. Islands close to the U.S. also gained. Grand Bahama, 50 miles distant, increased 32%. Customs duty on liquor brought about a situation like the Civil War period. The government once again became free of debt, civil service wages were raised, new government-financed hotels were built, and public services such as electricity, water, sewage, and roads were expanded.

The biggest profits were made by the Nassau merchants who controlled the government, known as "the Bay Street Boys." The 1920's was the era of the great Florida land boom and some of this spilled over into the Bahamas. Tiny Bimini, near Florida and a haunt of Ernest Hemmingway, became popular as a resort and achieved a hotel. Wealthy mainlanders became interested in acquiring their own "tropical island." Previously acrid, worthless "cays" had acquired value. The wealthy Bahamians, ever watchful for an opportunity to profit from changing world economic conditions, plowed their liquor profits into what most Bahamians still regarded as virtually worthless land.

The prototype land developer and promoter of tourism in the Bahamas is Harold G. Christie. Born in

31

Nassau in 1869, his fortune was made in the liquor trade
and consolidated in real estate. In 1927 he was elected
to the House of Assembly for Cat Island. He was one of
the founders in 1943 of Bahamas Airways and the first
chairman of the board of the Bahamas Government Development Board, later renamed the Ministry of Tourism, an
organization that into the 1960's spent a tenth of total
government revenue promoting the advantages of the
Bahamas to tourists, and more importantly, to foreign
investors. Like the other "Bay Street Boys", Christie's
contribution was not in developing land himself, but in
buying up many small parcels to combine into large parcels for wealthy foreigners. During the world depression of the 1930's and the unsettled years prior to
World War II, Christie persuaded two such foreigners to
come to the Bahamas whose substantial investments are
crucial to understanding the present: Harry Oakes and
Arthur Vining Davis.

Oakes was the larger of the two investors. His
fortune had been made from a gold mine he discovered in
Canada. Estimating that 85% of his income was being
taken from him in taxes, he emmigrated in 1934 to the
virtually tax-free Bahamas and bought 7,000 acres of
land on New Providence. Tax advantages to the wealthy
have remained an inducement to foreign investment into
the present times. Nine years after his arrival, Oakes
died in a still unsolved murder. During these years he
purchased the largest hotel in Nassau, built the first
airport, and became a member of the House of Assembly.
In his various enterprises, it is estimated that Oakes
provided steady employment for 1,500 laborers, paying
more than the prevailing minimum wage of four shillings
per day (Craton 1968:271). In light of the fact that
this was a period of world depression and the total
population of New Providence was less than 30,000, this
was a considerable contribution to the small economy.
Unlike the liquor trade and all the previous waves of
prosperity that had swept Nassau, the prosperity initiated by Oakes benefited the long-oppressed black majority of the population.

The steady jobs Oakes provided were augmented in
1942, when the United States, as a war measure, decided
to expand Oakes Airfield and build a new airbase at the
western end of New Providence. It was proposed that
2,400 Bahamian laborers be hired at the then prevailing
U.S. Negro wage rates, including a minimum wage of $2.00
per day. The Bahamas government, fearing that such

32

relatively high wages would bring economic chaos to the
colony, insisted that the minimum wage be four shillings
per day. Laborers quickly learned that while black
Bahamian truck drivers were earning one shilling per
hour, white U.S. Americans were earning $1.50 for the
same work. Less than a month after the start of construction, a riot occurred in which windows were broken
and stores looted in downtown Nassau for two days. Following this, minimum wages were raised. The 1942 riots
marked the beginning of the end of the Bay Street oli-
garchy. Further rioting has not occurred. The rise of
tourism in the Bahamas following World War II was accompanied by a rise in the income and political power of
the black majority. In 1967 the predominantly black
Progressive Liberal Party was voted into office. In
1973 the Bahamas ended its colonial ties with England,
becoming politically independent and a member of the
United Nations. Details of this major political transi-
tion are presented from an insider's point of view by
Doris L. Johnson in a book titled "The Quiet Revolution
in the Bahamas" (1972).

The pattern set in Nassau by Harry Oakes was dupli-
cated in all parts of the Bahamas by wealthy foreign
investors. One of the first to invest heavily in an
Out-Island was Arthur Vining Davis, chairman of the
board of Alcoa Aluminum and involved in many other business enterprises in the Pittsburgh area and in Florida.
Like Harry Oakes, Davis acquired land through Harold G.
Christie. Beginning with 5,000 acres north of Rock
Sound, Eleuthera in 1939, he eventually acquired about
30,000 acres, a majority of all the land in the South
Administrative District, the southern third of the
island. The venture known as South Eleuthera Properties
was a minor enterprise for Davis, but it had major repercussions for the small population of the district.

Older inhabitants still remember what the situation
was like in 1939. The main connection to the outside
world was a telegraph line to Governor's Harbour, in the
center of the island. Fortnightly a mail boat arrived
from Nassau. There was no electricity, no running water,
and very little in the way of motorized transport on the
barely passable roads. In this year and the following
Davis built two houses at what is now the Rock Sound
Club. Next he began clearing land for agriculture, pro-
posing to "root the rock," by breaking up the soft limestone as had been done with success in South Florida.
This enterprise required considerable local labor. For

the first time since the crash of the pineapple industry, steady wage labor became available in the district. People made a daily walk from as far as Deep Creek, twenty miles distant, to work in Davis' fields. By 1944 Davis had improved roads in the area, instituted more frequent boat service with his own "M. V. Rock Sound," arranged with Christie for twice-weekly flying boat service via Bahamas Airways, and introduced electricity and running water.

During the war years tomatos were produced on the land Davis had cleared. He built a canning factory in Rock Sound for this and other produce of the district. The present Rock Sound airport was begun in the early 1940's as a 1,200 foot strip for a crop dusting plane.

Following the war, Davis developed the area around his two houses into a fashionable resort, the Rock Sound Club. In cooperation with the government he extended roads, electricity, water, and telephone service in the district. In 1950, at the age of 84, he sold most of his holdings to the British Colonial Land Development Corporation. When that organization failed in 1954, Davis bought back most of his holdings at a profit. The agricultural area north of Rock Sound was sold to William Wood Prince, president of Chicago's Union Stockyards. Black Angus and Charolois breeding stock were raised there, cattle expensive enough to be flown from Eleuthera to various parts of Canada and the U.S. Some Eleutherans became cowboys.

Regaining his holdings south of Rock Sound, Davis began building a yacht harbor and golf course. The design and construction of the golf course were turned over to Trent Jones in exchange for beachfront land. Jones built some cottages here, the nucleus of the present Cotton Bay Club. In 1960 Davis, very advanced in years, sold his holdings to a friend of Trent Jones, Pan American's chairman-of-the-board, Juan Trippe.

In the 1960's expensive residences sprouted along the beach near the golf course of the very exclusive Cotton Bay Club.

Another posh residential area, Winding Bay, appeared north of the Rock Sound Club and a third resort, Island Inn, was built north of Winding Bay. Beginning in 1961, Pan American began daily service to Rock Sound, later expanded to twice daily during the winter months.

A flurry of development has occurred in the early
1970's. Most significant has been the start of a multi-
million dollar housing area on a 4,800 acre peninsula
formerly known as "Powell's Point," but now "Cape Eleuthera." In the summer of 1972 a golf course, a club-
house, a marina, villas for visiting land buyers, and
extensive road and utilities systems were nearing com-
pletion. Spurred by Cape Eleuthera, a small U.S. style
shopping center was built in Rock Sound, a new electrical generating plant was built, and work was underway
on a high school building in Rock Sound, the first high
school on Eleuthera.

The changes that have occurred in South Eleuthera
since 1939 are impressive, but merely a small part of
the Bahamian tourist boom that began after World War
II, due to ready accessibility of the islands by air-
plane. This development gained considerable momentum
during the 1960's. The increase in visitor arrivals
during this period is shown in Table 3-3. (Source:
Ministry of Tourism).

TABLE 3-3: VISITOR ARRIVALS

Year	Nassau	Freeport	Out-Islands	Total
1950	-	-	-	35,000
1960	305,553	-	36,424	341,977
1966	531,164	204,170	86,980	822,317
1968	664,755	332,026	75,423	1,072,213
1970	730,611	483,125	84,608	1,298,344
1972	941,533	483,872	86,453	1,511,858

The pioneering investments of Harry Oakes and A. V.
Davis were far overshadowed during the 1950's by Hunt-
ington Hartford's transformation of the small "Hog Cay"
that shelters Nassau's harbor into Miami Beach-like
"Paradise Island," and Wallace Grove's construction of
the American boomtown of Freeport in the previous wil-
derness of Grand Bahama Island. Limited to these two
places within the Bahamas are gambling casinos that
absorbed the trade from previous operations in Cuba.
Table 3-3 shows that the overwhelming number of tourists,
more than 90%, visit the two areas where casinos exist.
Referring back to Table 3-2 (page 30), it is evident
that the vast majority of postwar Bahamian population
growth has occurred in these same two places. The
facilities for the tourist boom in the Bahamas were
financed by the temporary condition of prohibition in

the United States. The boom itself seems to be founded on what may likewise prove to be a temporary condition: the illegality of casino gambling in all U.S. states except Nevada and New Jersey. According to government statistics, about 90% of the tourists come from the U.S., with Florida leading all the states. Once again, following the pattern evident throughout Bahamian history, it appears that what would be a minor change in the outside world, repeal of all or even some of the U.S. anticasino laws, could have catastrophic consequences in the unisolated, exposed Bahamas.

CHAPTER 5

CENSUS 1970

> With the coming of independence
> it is proposed that overseas missions
> shall be set up to represent the in-
> terests of the Bahamas in those coun-
> tries where we have significant inter-
> ests to pursue. Accordingly, a Baham-
> ian embassy will be founded in the
> first instance in Washington . . . .
> Consular offices will be established
> in New York and Miami where there are
> substantial Bahamian 'colonies' and
> which Bahamians visit in numbers
> (Pindling 1972: 26).

This chapter and the following three constitute a series of perspectives on the present human population of Eleuthera. This first member of the series views the island through the lenses of the latest census.

The April 1970 census of the Bahamas (Tertullien 1972) was unusually thorough in two respects. First, an attempt was made to complete census forms for every household and every individual resident of the country. Second, the 1970 census marked the entry of the Bahamas into the United Nationals World Census Program. This resulted in collection of a good deal of information beyond simple enumeration of the population, standard-ized data which can be compared with that of other na-tions participating in the program.

It is important to recognize that a long-standing census tradition regarding the island of Eleuthera is maintained in the 1970 census. "Eleuthera" refers to two administrative districts, the Governor's Harbour district in the center of the island and the Rock Sound district in the southern third. Northerly settlements on the island are grouped with small adjacent islands under the separate classification "Harbour Island and Spanish Wells." Using the census definition of "Eleu-thera," this chapter presents some basic facts about the island crucial to an understanding of its present system.

37

Table 4-1 presents a list of the settlements on Eleuthera and the population of each, arranged from north to south.

TABLE 4-1: POPULATION OF ELEUTHERAN SETTLEMENTS

Settlement	Males	Females	Total
Gregory Town	205	182	387
Alice Town & Hatchet Bay	381	405	786
James Cistern	186	199	385
Governor's Harbour	365	352	717
Palmetto Point	305	301	606
Savannah Sound	132	119	251
District Subtotal	1,574	1,558	3,132
Tarpum Bay	392	377	769
Rock Sound	481	464	945
Greencastle	212	226	438
Deep Creek	158	171	329
Weymss Bight	258	274	532
Bannerman Town	50	52	102
District Subtotal	1,551	1,564	3,115
Eleuthera Total	3,125	3,122	6,247

Table 4-1 confirms the point made in the chapter on ecology that Eleutheran settlements are dispersed according to the dictates of slash-and-burn agriculture. Size of the individual settlement appears to be directly related to the amount of opportunity for wage labor, as will be evidenced in Chapter Seven.

A second point to note in Table 4-1 is that the number of males and females in each of the settlements is approximately equal. This contrasts with the situation observed elsewhere in the Bahamas (Rogers 1965, Otterbein 1966), in the Afro-American Caribbean (Gonzales 1969), and in much of the developing world that a surplus of females, and resulting matrifocality, is found in outlying districts because males have gone to the metropolis to seek work.

A common index of matrifocality in a society is the percentage of households that are headed by females. The census indicates that of 1,417 heads of household on Eleuthera, 354 or 25% are female. This compares with recent figures of 10% among the U.S. white population, but 34% among U.S. blacks (U.S. Bureau of the

Census: 1974). A look at Eleutheran marital status by age group in Table 4-2 sheds some light on the reasons why 25% of Eleutheran households are female-headed. Widows constitute the largest component of female-headed households on the island, there being 172 widows in the population. Contrasting with other matrifocal societies, women separated from their husbands are a fairly small component, totaling only 63 in the Eleutheran population. More important than separated women are single women. Single women aged 35 and over are numerous enough in the Eleutheran population to account for the remaining 119 female-headed households.

TABLE 4-2:   ELEUTHERAN MARITAL STATUS BY AGE GROUP

(Figures express percent of row.)

Age	Sngl.	Married Legal	Married Com. Law	Widow Widwr.	Divrcd. Not Re-married	Seprtd.
0-14	100					
15-19	92	8				
20-24	48	49	1			1
25-29	31	65	2			2
30-34	13	75	4	2		6
35-39	12	75	5	2	1	5
40-44	9	75	5	4	2	10
45-49	9	75	3	6	1	6
50-54	8	78	1	9	1	2
55-59	14	69	3	9	3	1
60-64	4	76	2	11	1	
65-69	6	64	1	23	5	
70-74	12	62		25		1
75-79	6	50		44		
80-84	12	40		48		
85+	3	31		63		3

Since widowers, men separated from their wives, and single men are approximately equal in numbers to women of the same categories, it might be suspected that the seemingly high percentage of female-headed households is a result of a tendency toward single-person households. Census figures in Table 4-3 support this line of reasoning.

In the United States two-person households are the most frequent and three-person households exceed those of one person. In the United States the median age of

TABLE 4-3: ELEUTHERAN HOUSEHOLD SIZE

Number of Persons:	1	2	3	4	5	6	7
Number of Households:	288	273	164	144	131	112	100

Number of Persons:	8	9	10 plus
Number of Households:	65	58	114

marriage is 21 for females and 23 for males. Despite
increasing "serial monogamy," 75% of the U.S. population 18 and over is married (U.S. Census: 1970).
Relative to the U.S. the Eleutheran population shows a
greater tendency toward single-person households and a
greater tendency to marry late or not at all. The often
discussed tendency of Afro-Americans to engage in com-
mon-law marriage, while present on Eleuthera, is infre-
quent. Tables Three and Four indicate a tendency toward
personal autonomy among Eleutherans. Some suggestions
as to why this tendency exists are presented in the re-
mainder of this chapter. Further aspects of the characteristic and its implications are presented in succeeding chapters.

The population pyramid for Eleuthera, Table 4-4,
prompts two minor observations and shows one striking
feature. First, there seem to be a reasonable number
of people in the older age groups. To select only the
oldest category, those eighty and above, a total of 87
for a population of 6,247 seems quite respectable.
Longevity is slightly lower than in the U.S., but not
importantly so. Second, there are two minor fluctua-
tions in the curve. There appears to be an increment
to the population in the late twenties and early thir-
ties and another centering in the fifties. As will be
discussed shortly, the first bulge may be due largely
to immigration of laborers, the later one to immigration of employers and administrators.

The most striking feature of the population pyramid is the high percentage of people under age 16. The
"pyramid" for Eleuthera appears more like a tapering
candle set in a broad candleholder. 3,272 Eleutherans
of 6,247, or 52% are below 18. This compares with a
U.S. median age of 28.

Three explanations for the disproportionate number
of young people on Eleuthera can be suggested: a rapid
increase in the birth rate during the past sixteen years,
a rapid decrease in the death rate of young people during this period, and a traditional pattern of migration

TABLE 4-4:   ELEUTHERAN POPULATION PYRAMID

Age   Number

```
80 plus              57---------30
78-79                    11
76-77                   6--10
74-75                  13--13
72-73                  17---12
70-71                  10----28
68-69                  16----22
66-67                  21----22
64-65                 36------23
62-63                 27-------40
60-61                 44-------33
58-59                49--------32
56-57                50----------54
54-55                41---------46
52-53                49---------53
50-51                50----------61
48-49                40--------43
46-47                31--------50
44-45                43--------45
42-43               57----------41
40-41                49---------51
38-39                43--------45
36-37                51-----------56
34-35              67------------53
32-33              71-------------63
30-31              74--------------72
28-29             79---------------84
26-27           99------------------93
24-25              74---------------88
22-23            88----------------70
20-21            84---------------72
18-19            82---------------82
16-17              96--------------------124
14-15         153-----------------------------148
12-13       173----------------------------------167
10-11      185-----------------------------------167
 8- 9    212------------------------------------------203
 6- 7    207----------------------------------------------227
 4- 5    218----------------------------------------197
 2- 3    196----------------------------------------204
 0- 1    206-------------------------------------189
```

Males   Females

from the island at about age sixteen, the approximate age of leaving school. Available statistics seem to rule out the first two explanations. During the period 1953 to 1970, the Bahamian crude death rate per 1,000 was reduced from 12.2 to 6.2, but in the same period the crude birthrates per 1,000 dropped twice as much, from 37.6 to 25.2 (Tertullien 1971:26). Migration seems to be the explanation.

The 1970 census gives information on migration within the Bahamas and information on migration into the Bahamas from outside the country. 699 people are reported as having moved from Eleuthera to other islands of the Bahamas in the decade preceding the census. However, the number of migrants to Eleuthera exceeds the number who left. 643 people came to Eleuthera from elsewhere in the Bahamas. 519 people came from outside the Bahamas. The United States is the largest source of foreign immigration with 32%, followed by Haiti with 30%. The problem of the preponderance of young people in the population pyramid remains, but an important characteristic of the population has been established. Ten percent of the people are from outside the Bahamas. Roughly one person of five on the island of Eleuthera is not a native to the island.

An area where few statistics are available concerns migration of Bahamians to other countries. Through history there has been considerable migration from the Bahamas as well as into and within them. A circumstantial case can be made that recent migration from the Bahamas is high and increasing, paralleling the census statistics on migration within the Bahamas. Immigrants to the U.S.A. from the West Indies increased from 122,794 in the decade 1951-1960 to 519,499 in the decade 1961-1970. These figures do not include the U.S. possessions Puerto Rico and the Virgin Islands. If the major sources of West Indian immigration: Cuba, the Dominican Republic, and Jamaica are also subtracted, the smaller territories of the Caribbean contributed 26,010 in 1951-1960 and 97,603 in 1961-1970. (American Almanac 1974: 96). Expressed in absolute terms, these figures do not seem particularly high. Expressed as a percentage of total population, they gain in impressiveness. It has been estimated that net immigration to the United Kingdom from Jamaica during the decade 1953-1962 represented 9.7 percent of the remaining population (Tidrick 1966:29).

Figures for non-immigrant admission to the United

States from the Bahamas are astounding. In 1970, 101,739 Bahamians were admitted in this fashion. It appears to have been a record year. In 1960 the figure was 13,996, but in 1972 it was 84,372 (American Almanac 1974:99). Although there were certainly multiple entries by some persons, the 1970 figure represents 60% of all Bahamians, the 1972 figure 50%. Supported by the statement of the Prime Minister that there are substantial Bahamian colonies in the U.S. (Pindling 1972:26), and by frequent reference by Eleutherans to relatives and Bahamian friends in the U.S., these figures may provide the answer to the problem of the missing young adults of Eleuthera and elsewhere in the Bahamas. It would seem that a large percentage of Bahamians are temporarily in the United States. More important to the aim of understanding Eleutheran Bahamians, it would seem that these people are much more knowledgeable about the United States than vice versa.

A likely cause of migration is the search for wage labor. Tables 4-5 and 4-6 present the wage labor situation on Eleuthera as seen from the vantage of the 1970 census.

The eleven standard United Nations categories require some interpretation for the island of Eleuthera. In category two, the vast majority are engaged in the traditional type of agriculture, only 25 persons reporting their occupation as fishing. In category seven the vast majority of jobs are low-paid and seasonal in nature, e.g. maids, waiters, general laborers, cooks, launderers. Category ten includes many government jobs including a total of 115 teachers and assistant teachers.

The wage labor situation is seen from another perspective in Table 4-6.

This table shows that while 47% of the labor force is employees of private companies, only 1% is employers. This relationship reflects the fact that most jobs on the island are with very large companies such as previously discussed South Eleuthera Properties. Second only to employees of private companies in the working labor force, are "own-account workers." Farmers account for a large portion of this group, but it includes everyone who earns money in an independent fashion: keepers of small stores, seamstresses, fishermen. The size of this group, 17% of the male labor force and 11% of the total work force, buttresses the impression

43

TABLE 4-5: ELEUTHERANS AGED 14 AND OVER BY
ECONOMIC ACTIVITY

Economic Activity	Total #	Total %	Males #	Males %	Females #	Females %
1.Unemployed-student schoolboy/girl house-wife, retired, of independent means	1159	33	253	15	906	51
2.Agriculture, hunting, forestry & fishing	453	13	211	12	142	8
3.Mining and quarrying	1	-	1	-	-	-
4.Manufacturing	56	2	37	2	19	1
5.Electricity, gas and water	38	1	37	2	1	-
6.Construction	223	6	216	13	7	-
7.Wholesale and retail trade, restaurants, and hotels	723	21	397	23	326	18
8.Transport, storage and communication	129	4	93	5	36	2
9.Financing, insurance, real estate, and business services	45	1	33	2	12	1
10.Community, social & personal services	456	13	236	14	220	12
11.Employed (or unem-ployed for health or other reasons) but economic activity not given	213	6	114	7	99	6
Total	3496	100	1728	100	1768	100

TABLE 4-6: ELEUTHERANS AGED 14 AND OVER BY
ECONOMIC STATUS

Economic Status	Total #	Total %	Males #	Males %	Females #	Females %
1.Employee (Private Co.)	1632	47	1014	59	618	35
2.Employee (Government or Public Corporation)	267	8	144	8	123	7
3.Employer	21	1	19	1	2	-
4.Own Account Worker	401	11	291	17	110	6
5.Unpaid Family Worker	16	-	7	-	9	-
6.Unemployed-student, housewife, retired, of independent means	1159	33	253	15	906	51
Total	3496	100	1728	100	1768	100

TABLE 4-7:   ELEUTHERAN HOUSEHOLD INCOME DISTRIBUTION

Income (B$)	Nil-2000	2001 5000	5001 10000	10001 15000	15001 20000	20001 & over	Total
#Households	585	506	240	74	22	10	1434
%Households	41	35	17	5	1	1	100

(Bahamian dollars are approximately par with U.S. dollars).

gained earlier from marriage statistics and household size that personal autonomy is an Eleutheran trait.

Personal autonomy, including a willingness to migrate within the Bahamas and to the United States, would appear to be fostered by conditions on the island, particularly the condition which is the theme of this work: that the island is not a self-sufficient, isolated paradise. It was suggested earlier that with sufficient income, it could be such a paradise. Table 4-7 shows the 1970 household income distribution of Eleutherans.

Although these household income figures greatly exceed those of many other nations of the world and even of the Caribbean, the indicated median household income of about $3,000. places the majority of Eleutherans in what the U.S. government considers poverty. This low income, coupled with tremendous exposure to the United States through tourists and investors, considerably above the U.S. income average, and exposure through radio, movies, magazines, and television would seem to explain the Eleutheran urge to migrate in search of higher income. Such low income, coupled with such exposure to higher income might prompt an opposite question: Why do Eleutherans remain on the island? Some possible answers are suggested in the final chapter of this work.

This chapter has presented a view of the present population of Eleuthera that emerges from tabulation of census returns. As will be indicated shortly, this view is somewhat distorted. Nonetheless, the census presents basic information, important as context to the following more focused, but narrower views of the population based on fieldwork.

One way to summarize the census information is to
suggest that despite considerably changed world conditions and outward appearances, the present situation on
the island is similar in basic ways to what it was three
hundred years ago: settlements are small and dispersed;
as was the case in the early years and through its history, there is considerable movement of people to and
from the island, especially from the island; "freedom,"
the original reason for settlement, remains high as
regards personal autonomy, but low as regards freedom
from physical want.

CHAPTER 6

THE HUMAN SYSTEM

That's it. That's the chief humbug
'around here. People don't cooperate.

Tourists? We like them more than we
like each other.

(Fragments of island conversation.)

According to anthropological axiom human popula-
tions are more than "things," single entities to be
described and measured from the outside with census-
takers' calipers. They are systems, consisting of different parts that interrelate in such a way that a
change in one of the parts effects the whole system.
The intent of this chapter is to examine how the circumstances of exposure on Eleuthera, the theme of this work,
affects the working of the social system on the island.
The chapter proceeds by examining the ways Eleutherans
and subgroups of Eleutherans say, "We are different."

The attitude that "we are different" is expressed
in multitudinous ways. Although few Bahamians would
pass up a chance to possess the wealth of U.S. tourists
and the current generation is attempting with considerable success to emulate the U.S. standard and style of
living, there is a general feeling that money has moral-
ly corrupted many U.S. tourists. Tourists frequently
behave in ways that contradict even their own moral
standards at home. Perhaps more perplexing to Bahamians,
they seem to have very little sense of religion. "Having a good time" can be understood and even readily
joined into by Bahamians, but the seeming rush toward
damnation cannot be fathomed.

Toward England the attitude is more complex. Being
a British colony from its inception until July, 1973,
the entire way of life is to a considerable degree derived from England. Thus the Bahamian attitude is similar
to that of the United States. A major difference is
that separation from the "mother country" is a current
event in the Bahamas. There are considerable feelings
of insecurity due to a perceived threat from Cuba to the
small population of the Bahamas and due to conscious
realization of economic dependence on the world system.
Feelings of insecurity ran so high on the island of

47

Abaco, strong in Loyalist heritage, that Abaco attempted to secede from the Bahamas during the independence movement in order to remain a British colony.

Outside observers often see one general Afro-American culture in the Caribbean (Wagley 1960, Whitten and Szwed 1970). From the vantage of an island within the Caribbean one sees diversity. For Eleuthera and the Bahamas, the emphasis on differences between Caribbean nations is well exemplified in attitudes toward Jamaicans versus attitudes toward Haitians. Often coming from the University of the West Indies, Jamaicans found in the Bahamas tend to exceed the local population in education and in specialized job skills, such as nursing. They have money and prestige, tending to be regarded in the same light as U.S. citizens. Haitians, on the other hand, arrive in the Bahamas more to escape poverty than to market specialized skills.. Speaking a different language and with little schooling, they readily accept the hard manual labor Bahamians prefer to avoid. Keeping to themselves in most cases, they are generally looked down upon, but nonetheless regarded with a certain awe. Seemingly always cheerful, they are regarded as clever entrepreneurs. The author was told that if one gives a Haitian ten dollars to do a job, he will find another who will do it for five dollars and pocket the difference. Perhaps it is this cleverness attributed to them and willingness to tolerate hard and tedious work, combined with a Bahamian love of clothing, that has allowed Haitians virtually to monopolize the occupation of tailor on Eleuthera and generally to function in the society despite being stigmatized.

Residents of an island seem to distrust the residents of even nearby other islands. Although Abaco's recent attempt to secede from the Bahamas failed, two small islands successfully seceded from the Bahamas in 1848 and established themselves as a separate colony: the Turks and Caicos Islands. The failure of the British West Indies Federation (Domingo 1956, Springer 1967) was brought to world attention in 1967 when British paratroopers landed on tiny Anguilla Island, population 6,000, in an unseccessful attempt to prevent it from disaffiliating with nearby St. Kitts. It would seem that pride in one's own island and xenophobia of even nearby other islands are widespread in the Caribbean.

On Eleuthera, the author once witnessed a half

hour's animated discussion of the relative quality of
workmanship in house construction by men from Nassau
versus men from Eleuthera. Whatever the actual differences in workmanship, the sophisticated and worldlywise
Nassau men lost the debate, being outnumbered by the
Eleutherans and not on their home turf.

Social distinctions based on skin color are so
prevalent throughout the world that it would be surprising to find such distinctions missing on Eleuthera and
in the Bahamas. It is a serious mistake, however, to
assume that relations between the races are identical
to those in the United States. Three very important
differences are apparent. First, the black population
vastly outnumbers the white. Statistics on racial composition are not presently kept, but estimates place
whites at less than 15% (Sharer 1955:14). Second, on
Eleuthera and in the out-islands there have not been
great differences in wealth between whites and blacks.
During times of hardship both groups have suffered considerably. If at present the average wealth of whites
is slightly higher than blacks, there is a considerable
overlap in the ranges of distribution: there are many
quite well-to-do black Eleutherans and many quite poor
whites.

In Nassau, and therefore the national scene, the
situation has been different until recently. Bahamian
wealth and the government are controlled until 1967 by
elite whites. With the "quiet revolution" (Johnson
1972) came a third major factor making race relations
different and much less tension-ridden than elsewhere:
the Prime Minister and most of the officials and func-
tionaries of the government are now black, reflecting
the population of the Bahamas.

Most of the settlements in the out-islands of the
Bahamas are entirely black in population. A scattered
few, such as Spanish Wells, off the north coast of
Eleuthera, are entirely white in population. Of the
three settlements in the Rock Sound district, "South
Eleuthera," that were examined in detail for this study,
only Rock Sound has any whites. Here they are about
ten percent of the population. A large portion moved
to Rock Sound from nearby Powell's Point, now Cape
Eleuthera, at the time that land was bought for A. V.
Davis. Virtually all the Rock Sound whites are Metho-
dists, and sit together during services toward the front
of the church.

49

The situation in church symbolizes the usual position of whites in the social structure of Rock Sound:
equal but very definitely separate. Whites interact
without rancor with blacks on a formal, polite, business-
like basis. With few exceptions there is no social visiting, close friendship, marriage, or mutual attendance
at social events such as softball games, beach parties,
and dances. Only one type of social event draws whites
as well as blacks. This is any public performance by
schoolchildren, usually as part of the national holiday
or church festivity.

The general pattern of rigid separation of the
races is contradicted by a few young adult males an outsider would consider white. These few form most of their
intimate associations, including sexual partners and
wives, with blacks. One of these told the author he
feels he is neither white nor black, and it really makes
no difference what color a person's skin is. Perhaps
persons such as this are effectively engaged on Eleuthera
in creating a world where skin color does not matter.
Perhaps attendance by both groups at performances by
schoolchildren indicates the parents' desire for the
children to mix freely. But at present, in a way different from in the United States, skin color seems to
matter very much on Eleuthera and in the Bahamas.

Since they are isolated from each other geographically and are low in economic interdependence, the individual settlements develop distinct cultures. In the
schools children will often ridicule the dialect of a
newcomer from a settlement only ten miles distant. It
is generally agreed that people in other settlements
have not only different ways of speaking, but different
ways of behaving and thinking. From the Rock Sound
point of view people in Bannerman Town are poverty-
striken farmers, to be pitied because they are honest
and hard working. People in Greencastle are wild,
fighting all the time, and to be avoided. Exceptions
are recognized, but the stereotypes exist.

The well-developed sense of membership in a speci-
fic settlement is most conspicuous at softball games.
On Eleuthera every settlement possessing the requisite
number of young players fields a softball team. Many
of the games are never completed because fights break
out over calls that would merely be grumbled about in
the United States. At any victory there is a great
celebration by the winning team. When a small settle-

ment beats a larger opponent, the celebration may extend
for hours.

Considering one's own settlement to be distinct in
culture from other settlements leads to the major social
division within each settlement, that between natives,
those born and raised in the settlement, and non-natives.
It will be recalled that approximately one resident in
five on Eleuthera is not native to the island. This
number of non-natives in each settlement is augmented
by Eleutherans from other settlements who have moved
for reasons of work or marriage. Natives are well aware
of who is and who is not native. The topic frequently
comes up in conversation and natives can quickly and
easily specify the category of any household in the
settlement. Non-natives, on the other hand, can frequently be heard to complain that despite years of living in a settlement, they do not feel accepted by those
who were born and raised there.

This review of ways in which Eleutherans say "we
are different" reveals quite a multitude and suggests
that a prime characteristic of this small society is
social fragmentation: people tend to emphasize differences between themselves and others more than similari-
ties and do not readily organize in cohesive groups.

Eleutherans generally concur with this view of
their social system. It has been indicated that non-
natives frequently complain about feelings of not being
accepted by natives. Natives also bemoan a lack of
social solidarity, but often feel that it is caused by
too many outsiders. At the opening of this chapter the
first two "fragments of island conversation" are from
astute native observers of the local social scene and
are further direct evidence that Eleutherans recognize
social fragmentation in their social system and view it
as a problem. Just as the original motto of the Bahamas
expressed a desire for commerce, the new motto also
appears to express a desire rather than an actual state
of affairs. Its phrasing is: "FORWARD, UPWARD, ONWARD
TOGETHER."

A strong case can be made that Eleutheran society
has been socially fragmented from its beginnings because
this trait has proved adaptive to the exposed circumstances of the island. The true beginnings of Eleutheran and Bahamian society are, of course, the Lucayan
branch of the Arawak tribes. All evidence indicates

51

that each village among them was an independent political unit, that no village exceeded fifteen houses in
size and many consisted of but one house, a single family
(Craton 1968:23-24).

It will be recalled that the original settlement
of the Eleutheran Adventurers quickly fragmented into
two presumably widely separated settlements soon after
it was founded. Perhaps initiated merely by a "quirk
of history," personality differences between two leaders,
the split proved useful because more of the thin and
dispersed resources of land and sea could be exploited
by two small settlements than by one large one. The
colony was augmented in its early years by the forced
passage of Bermudan undesirables: political dissidents,
unruly slaves, and all free slaves. If these people
were undesirable on Bermuda they were probably equally
so on Eleuthera, supporting the idea that further small
settlements were established in these very early years.
Within seventeen years, a second island, New Providence,
was settled.

With the coming of piracy to the New Providence
settlement of Nassau, there was a revolutionary shift
in the social system of. the Bahamas. Prior to this time
each settlement had been autonomous because each had
essentially the same economy consisting of slash-and-
burn agriculture plus fishing for food, and a multitude
of activities that could collectively be labled "scrounging" for the financial income that was necessary in this
outpost of European society. With the coming of piracy,
non-agriculturalists quickly exceeded the capacity of
the small island (greatest dimensions: twenty-one miles
by seven miles) to feed them. The settlements of Eleuthera gained a steady source of income through selling
any food they could produce beyond their immediate needs.
The two islands thus developed a relationship of mutual
interdependence, New Providence bringing cash and pro-
ducts from the outside world into the system, Eleuthera
supplying food. The pineapple boom of the late nineteenth century allowed Eleuthera to almost equal New
Providence in population because the island was feeding
the wider world. When the boom ended, the population
dropped and Eleuthera reverted to its traditional way
of life: what might be called "subsistence-plus" agriculture and fishing. Through history the Eleutheran
settlements have developed links to Nassau and the outside world rather than to each other. The fragmented
nature of Eleutheran society, first witnessed among

the founders of the colony, continues into the present.

But why does this social fragmentation continue into the present? Eleuthera has seen a quarter century of land development and tourism leading to the 1970 census report that only 13% of the population is now engaged in producing food (Table 4-5, page 44). According to the 1970 census most Eleutherans are now engaged in specialized occupations directly or indirectly related to the tourist industry. To view the occupational statistics in this abstract way divorces them from their Eleutheran, "exposed island," context and makes them misleading.

Just how they are misleading is pointed out in a recent article by Lambros Comitas titled: "Occupational Multiplicity in Rural Jamaica" (1973). When Comitas went to Jamaica he carried with him a typology of three types of rural society that had been posited for the Caribbean region from the massive cultural-ecological study, "The People of Puerto Rico" (Steward et al 1956). The first type is plantation workers, landless wage employees attached to large-scale agricultural organizations geared to the production and marketing of an export crop for market. The second is farmers, agricultural entrepreneurs who own land, hire wage labor or depend on sharecroppers or tenants for the cultivation of commercial crops. The third, peasants, agricultural producers, distinct from fishermen, who retain control of land and who aim at subsistence, not reinvestment. For each of these types a different social structure is posited (Padilla 1960).

Studying Jamaica, an island more richly endowed with resources than the Bahamas, but sharing the same British cultural substructure, Comitas finds that about 75% of the population is rural and 25% of the total population fits the social-economic type, "Plantation worker." However, for the remaining 50% of Jamaicans: "most members of this rural population segment fit into neither the farmer nor the peasant category" (1973:160). To explain this Comitas asserts:

> Rural Jamaicans found it necessary
> to combine several economic activities
> in order to subsist (and) developed a
> way of life based on a system of occu-
> pational multiplicity which maximizes
> as well as protects their limited

economic opportunities and which in
turn influences the nature of their
social alignments and organization
(1973: 163-164).

This conclusion was reached in a study for the
Jamaican government intended to promote the formation
of fishing cooperatives in five ostensibly "fishing"
settlements. Comitas found that the settlements ranged
widely in the actual amount of time devoted to fishing,
but more pertinent to the major point of his paper,
"except for one specialized settlement, from 63 to 79
percent of all males gainfully occupied are engaged in
more than one economic activity" (1973: 165). In the
area of Jamaica he studied, like Eleuthera, the possible
economic activities are six: subsistence cultivator,
commercial agriculturalist, wage laborer, own-account
artisan or tradesman, subsistence fisherman, and commercial fisherman. As is the case on Eleuthera, many
Jamaicans engage in more than two of the alternatives.

Comitas sees consequences of occupational multiplicity for the social system that are strongly reminiscent
of Eleuthera:

> This requires decisions as to work
> priorities and work schedules and ties
> individuals to a convoluted set of so-
> cial obligations . . . essentially lat-
> eral ones connecting members of the
> same stratum . . . interaction between
> these strata and the superordinate strata
> of the total Jamaican society tends to
> remain minimal and fragmentary . . .
> The internal rationality of such a con-
> fined system is self evident to its
> participants. A socio-economic balance
> is achieved which offers maximum secur-
> ity with minimum risk, in a basically
> limited environment. As the advantages
> are clear, so are the disadvantages:
> competition for scarce resources within
> a finite area engenders tension and an
> emotionally disruptive atmosphere;
> social mobility is structurally hindered;
> capital accumulation is difficult; tech-
> nological levels tend to remain rudimen-
> tary and communication with other seg-
> ments of the society is incomplete and

imprecise . . . Clearly much more work
and analysis is needed before a reasonable level of comprehension is reached.
For the purposes of social-scientific
research in the Caribbean, however, the
·identification and understanding of such
population segments in an area noted for
lack of extensive kin networks and relatively weak community organization is
especially pertinent and should prove of
heuristic value (1973: 171-173, emphasis
added).

Due to occupational multiplicity it is a mistake
to interpret occupational statistics for Eleuthera in
the same way one would interpret those of the United
States. On Eleuthera much more than 13 percent of the
population is engaged in food production. In the smaller settlements, such as Bannerman Town, it is the main
but not sole occupation of virtually everyone, male and
female. In medium-sized settlements, such as Greencastle,
it is a main occupation of a large portion of the people.
In the largest settlement on the island, Rock Sound,
there are a few people whose sole occupation is farming,
but examination of the vegetation surrounding the settlement shows that the region is as intensively farmed as
that surrounding any other settlement. The majority of
Rock Sound farmers are thus people who devote only a
small portion of their time to it.

When the census taker came around the question was:
"What was your main occupation in the last six months."
It is probably safe to say that many people whose pri-
mary occupation is farming replied by naming an activity
at which they spent a smaller portion of their time because, first, most farming activity is subsistence oriented and thus does not count as an occupation; and
second, farming is low prestige work and people would
prefer to name something else.

The important point is that the settlements of
Eleuthera have been and are to a considerable, if somewhat varying, degree characterized by occupational multiplicity. Although there is a slightly higher degree
of occupational specialization in the larger settlements,
many of even the most prosperous people there are engaged in two or more very different economic activities.
On the island even a seemingly specialized occupation,
such as "construction worker," can be seen as multiplex

relative to highly industrialized societies. A worldly-wise Rock Sound construction worker observed: "Even though wages are lower here, the labor charges for building a house would be about the same as in the States because there you have one guy who just hangs doors all day long and gets very good at it. Another guy just paints the inside walls. Here, one man has to do all the jobs."

On Eleuthera, Jamaica, and perhaps many other islands occupational multiplicity has developed as a means of exploiting sparce resources. The less erudite word used to describe earlier Eleutheran activities was "scrounging." Avoiding the problems of "having all one's eggs in one basket," scrounging creates a situation in which everyone tends to be engaged in all activities, thus competitive and socially fragmented. Due to the exposed nature of island life, the systemic articulations of islanders tend to be stronger with outside systems than within the island subsystem.

CHAPTER 7

OUTWARD APPEARANCES

WHERE ARE THE PALM TREES?
·(Disappointed first reaction of a
U.S. college student arriving at
Rock Sound).

In the summers of 1969 and 1970 there was a financial inducement for a tourist to fly to Rock Sound,
Eleuthera. If one flew Pan American from Miami or New
York to Nassau, there was no additional charge for the
short hop from Nassau to Rock Sound. With the emergence
of the Cape Eleuthera development, traffic had increased
enough by 1972 for a fare to be applied to the fifteen
minute flight and for the service to be financially in
the black.

Since visitors may clear customs at Rock Sound, the
airport there is technically "Rock Sound International
Airport." Just as luggage bound for Chicago bears a
tag labeled "CHI," that bound for Rock Sound is labeled
"RSD." Despite being fully incorporated in the international system, it is difficult to envision a smaller or
less bustling international airport. There is one run-
way, oriented into the prevailing northeasterly winds.
Although a giant Boeing 747 is reported to have landed
at Rock Sound shortly after some of these were acquired
by Pan American, the usual pattern is for one Boeing 707
to arrive and depart daily, two during the height of the
winter tourist season. In addition to the commercial
jets, a few private planes arrive, usually owned not by
temporary tourists but by wealthy members of the Cotton
Bay Club. According to government statistics, commercial flights to Rock Sound average ten per week, private
flights eight per week. The airport building is about
half the size of a typical U. S. supermarket, constructed of concrete block. The waiting room is quite crow-
ded if more than twenty passengers assemble there.

Despite its unimposing appearance by world standards, the Rock Sound airport is a fitting place to begin
this chapter, for it is the usual point of arrival and
the intent of this chapter is to take a verbal tour of
South Eleuthera, the Rock Sound District. ₁This is not
a tourist tour. Tourists rush to the self-contained
enclaves of the resort developments and emerge only to
leave the island. Regarding the resort developments as

57

important context, this tour visits three settlements, settlements selected to represent the range of variation on the island in size and modernity. This chapter adds descriptive detail to generalizations presented in previous chapters, but its major purpose is to set the stage for the succeeding chapter in which an important question is considered: As the outward circumstances of human communities change from traditional to modern, must there be a corresponding change in the people themselves, in their values and attitudes?

Nowadays virtually everyone who enters or leaves South Eleuthera passes through the Rock Sound airport. The three weekly "mailboats" that haul freight to and from the island are an alternative for passengers, but are seldom used because they are regarded as unclean and unreliable. Inter-island travel by private boat is surprisingly sparse. During three summers of fieldwork only three tourist yachts were observed in the Rock Sound harbour and there was no indication that any Eleutheran visited another island or even another settlement on the same island by boat. Very occasionally fishermen from Nassau can be observed in Eleutheran waters in search of the Bahamian delicacy: conch.

Aside from its importance as the link between South Eleuthera and the outside world, the airport is one of many sources of wage labor for the people of Rock Sound. Jobs range over a spectrum from airport manager to customs and immigration officers, ticket sales, taxi and car rental, baggage handlers, and the operator of a small concession stand.

The airport is perhaps most important in a symbolic sense. It is owned and operated by Pan American World Airways. Since the Eleutheran holdings of A. V. Davis were purchased by Pan American's founder, Juan Trippe, it can be said that Pan American symbolizes the major economic force in the small economy of South Eleuthera. Technically, the force is "the South Eleuthera Group of Companies." Most Eleutherans refer to it simply as "the company."

The center of Rock Sound is located about a mile and a half south of the airport. Within a short distance from the airport one encounters a series of houses constructed in U. S. Suburban "ranch" style, made of concrete block with picture windows, sliding glass doors, air conditioners, and TV antennas. These are part of the latest "concentric circle" of housing in Rock Sound, constructed within the past decade. A few more such houses are to be found at the southern extremity of the settlement, but most are located in the eastern sector. In these areas the casual observer is led to believe he is in a situation equivalent to a U. S. suburb. The casual observer is not aware that the interior furnishings are usually spartan relative to U. S. expectations for the housing style, that the air conditioner is seldom used because electricity is generated from diesel fuel and thus very expensive, that the TV antenna is connected to a small-screen black and white model if it is even connected. Since the nearest station is 250 miles away in Miami, reception is poor and some owners have gotten rid of the set but "haven't gotten around" to taking down the antenna. In summary, the newer housing of Rock Sound indicates a patterning after current U. S. styles, with emphasis on externals, since the complete package is financially out of reach.

About halfway between the airport and the geographic center of Rock Sound is a newly constructed shopping center, again in U. S. suburban fashion. This two-building complex was constructed in 1971, simultaneous with the onset of construction for the $30 million Cape Eleuthera housing development. One building houses a branch of Chase Manhattan Bank. The other is a line of five stores: a small supermarket, a hardware store, an auto parts store, one vacant store, and a beauty parlor. The shopping center and the first three stores listed are owned and operated by the company. They were formerly housed in older buildings to the south, where the main company offces are still located.

The next notable location encountered is the wire-fenced equipment yard of the company. Here one sees rusting iron boilers, boat hulls, a wide variety of old trucks and bulldozers. Until recently, a steady hum emanated from a building here housing electrical generators for the district, but this was moved in the early 1970's to a modern steel-frame building north of the airport. The move coincided with the establishment of Cape Eleuthera and expansion of generating capacity.

A short distance further takes one into the old section of the settlement. Within this area most houses were built prior to the era of tourism and are of wood-frame construction. The houses are located much closer to one another, some are quite dilapidated and a few abandoned.

59

MAP 3: ROCK SOUND

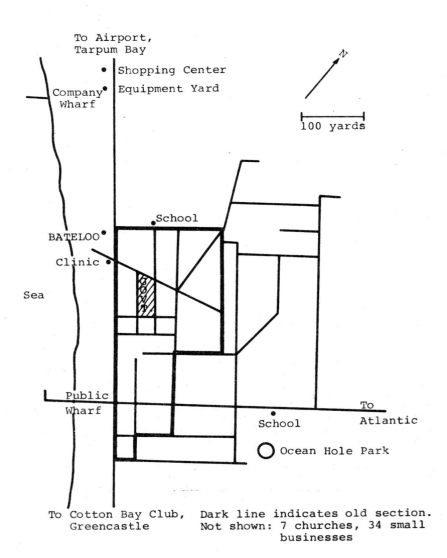

To Airport,
Tarpum Bay

Shopping Center

Company   Equipment Yard
Wharf

100 yards

School

BATELOO

Clinic

Sea

Public
Wharf

To
School   Atlantic

Ocean Hole Park

To Cotton Bay Club,   Dark line indicates old section.
   Greencastle   Not shown: 7 churches, 34 small
                              businesses

With entry into the old section comes a feeling
that one is in a foreign country, not merely a U. S.
suburb. The change is more than architectural. From
the airport to this point the landscape has been domi-
nated by evidences of the company: the airport, the
shopping center, the equipment yard, even the houses,
built primarily from earnings from company induced tourism. In the old section one enters the geographical
domain of the second largest employer in South Eleuthera,
the government. The first government edifice to be encountered is a small building with a substantial steel
tower behind it, supporting a large dish-shaped antenna
directed westerly toward Nassau. This is the headquarters for South Eleuthera of BATELCO, the government-
operated telephone and telegraph company. It serves
the 90 telephones in Rock Sound and one telephone in
each of the other settlements of the district. As a
vivid example of increasing interlinkage, the Bahamas
recently received its own telephone area code (809),
and the telephones of Rock Sound are now incorporated
within the direct-distance dialing system of the United
States.

At the next intersection one encounters the government operated "clinic." This is the medical center for
South Eleuthera. It houses the government doctor and
nurses, who visit the other settlements on a weekly
basis.

Set back from the main road, one block east of the
clinic is the government administrative center, an im-
posing two-story building with the house of the district
commissioner, the chief governmental official, adjacent.
On the ground floor of this building is the post office
and the office of the immigration officer. On the second
floor are the offices of the district commissioner and
a room where the commissioner holds court once or more
a week. Behind the administrative building, to the east,
are buildings housing a police station and a jail.
About half a dozen policemen trained in Nassau are ap-
pointed to South Eleuthera and stationed in Rock Sound.
They support local constables in each of the settlements.

A U. S. observer is accustomed to looking for the
"center of town," a "downtown" district where business,
government, industry, and entertainment facilities are
concentrated, with housing relegated to the periphery
of this central area. Perhaps reflective of the social
fragmentation discussed in the preceding chapter, the
settlements of Eleuthera have no center.

61

With a population of 945, Rock Sound is the largest settlement not only in South Eleuthera, but on the entire island. Its size would appear to be related to the fact that it is the district headquarters for "the company" and the government, and thus has the greatest employment opportunities of any settlement. Although these two large economic entities are somewhat concentrated geographically, they are concentrated in different parts of the settlement. The remaining sources of non-agricultural income: small stores, bars and restaurants, auto repair facilities and gas stations, barber shops, a tailor shop, a bakery, and a small concrete-block factory are scattered seemingly randomly amidst houses throughout the settlement.

The opposite of Rock Sound in size and in opportunity for wage labor is the smallest settlement of the island, Bannerman Town, 1970 population 102, located twenty miles south of Rock Sound near the southern tip of the island. Midway between these two extremes geographically and in size of the economy is Greencastle, 1970 population 438. It is possible to travel by road from Rock Sound to Bannerman Town without passing through Greencastle. This route will be followed in the verbal tour so that midpoint of size and modernity can be considered in relation to the extremes.

About a mile south of Rock Sound one loses sight of the sea and enters the bush. A view of the sea is not again encountered from the main road until one reaches the very southernmost tip of the island. Undoubtedly as a defense against theft, very few farmer's fields are visible from the road. The drive through this "natural" vegetation of Eleuthera contrasts markedly with preconceptions of the tropical isle. A botanist will recognize a variety of species, but to the untrained observer, it appears to be a monotonous dense thorniness. About eight miles south of Rock Sound the bush is temporarily replaced by low, marshy vegetation as the road crosses an area only a few feet above sea level. If there has been a rain recently, the road will be covered with water. At the end of this stretch, a mile north of Greencastle, there is a road leading to the left and a sign announcing: "Cotton Bay Club."

Turning to the left the vegetation immediately changes. The bush is gone, replaced by preconceived "tropical" vegetation: palm trees, poinciana trees in orange-red splendor, bougainvilla, jasmine, and between them, grass instead of tne usual limestone. People are frequently seen walking the two-mile stretch of road between Greencastle and the Cotton Bay Club. In the summer, these people are likely to consist mainly of the agents of ecological transformation: groundskeepers and gardeners. Although these people have the lowest paying jobs at the club, the jobs are the most secure because they are needed throughout the year. Informants estimate that about thirty people are employed at the club during the summer, sixty during the winter. Since this is a very exclusive private club, membership lists are not available. Local estimates range from 200 to 300 members.

Less than a mile after turning into the club, one encounters the golf course. In the summer, the grass is almost always brown, revealing yet another way in which Eleuthera is not the lush, tropical paradise of island myth. With an average elevation of less than twenty feet above sea level, fresh water cannot be as abundant as it is in continental areas. The fresh water that is available has precolated through the limestone to sealevel, and although heavier than sea water, rests on top of it in "lenses." That these lenses can be depleted easily is attested to by more than the summer appearance of the golf course. The drinking water in Rock Sound frequently has a strong taste of salt. School children are told not to drink it. This means buying bottled water, or more likely a trip to transport water from another settlement where it may be more abundant. The government owns a water tank truck that is in frequent use transporting water to all the settlements including tiny Bannerman Town. Recognition of the water problem is incorporated in the plans for the latest tourist development, Cape Eleuthera. Two very large water towers are erected on the golf course there, enabling periods of relatively abundant water to be extended into the periods of drought. Also, home builders will be encouraged not to have lawns and gardens, but to leave most of their acreage in the existing bush.

Moving from the Cotton Bay golf course toward the Atlantic coast a dune of sand about fifty feet in elevation is encountered. This dune extends the entire length of South Eleuthera. Its mode of construction is readily apparent. Driven by the prevailing northeasterly winds, the waves of the Atlantic pound over a reef about a thousand yards from the coast then roll on to the shore. Looking due east, one recollects that the next landfall

would be Africa. The waves rolling in here have had
considerable distance to build momentum. Beachcombers
prize glass fishnet floats carried here from the other
side of the Atlantic and attempt to overlook plastic
bottles and other debris of more recent vintage carried
perhaps an equal distance.

On top of the dune one encounters about two dozen
houses built of concrete block in the style encountered
in Rock Sound. The interiors are more sumptuous than
in Rock Sound, but with a few exceptions, wealth does
not seem to be on display here. The names of the owners
are familiar in the U. S. worlds of business and government. This is a place where such people come to escape
the urban-industrial ratrace. With sufficient financial resources, they are able to create the environment
of the tropical isle.

The summer hurricane season finds the Cotton Bay
Club closed and virtually deserted. Nassau is affected
by a hurricane about once every five years and hit severely every ten or fifteen years. The rate is approximately the same on nearby Eleuthera. Like the Cotton
Bay Club, most tourist developments are constructed on
the sand dune on the windward and therefore sandy shore
of the island. The native settlements are built on the
leeward, rocky shore of the island, facing the more
placid waters of Exuma Sound. It would seem that the
native settlement pattern is an adaptation to hurricanes.
Loss of a house at the Cotton Bay Club would be a minor
matter to most of the owners. They have the resources
to fly in the face of nature. Native Eleutherans, with
fewer resources, are less insulated from these forces.

The tour of the Cotton Bay Club is quickly completed. South of the houses is an unostentatious club-
house with swimming pool surrounded by about a dozen
"villas," small, unimposing structures, but well-appoin-
ted and well-kept for members of the club who have not
built homes and for guests of members.

Following the loop of road that passes through the
club, one quickly reenters the predominant bush and
rejoins the main Eleutheran road south of Greencastle.
The ten-mile trip south to Bannerman Town is usually
unmarked by an encounter with another vehicle because
there are only three or four autos and a couple of small
trucks in that entire settlement. It is easy to achieve
a feeling of quiet, peaceful solitude and closeness to

nature. In such a mood the uninitiated might easily miss both turnoffs to Bannerman Town and drive on to the southern tip of the island, unaware of either the settlement or its ancient resource, an area of perhaps 100 acres cleared for the commercial production of pineapple.

The author, accompanied by two of his students, did just this on his first trip to Bannerman Town. About a mile from the southern tip of the island, the paving on the main road ends and one must slowly negotiate a rough trail of limestone and sand. One finally arrives at a hill on top of which is an old building of crude mortar that served as a lighthouse in bygone days. Next to it is an automatic light on a metal pole. Isolated as this windswept spot might seem, that light is part of an international system and is indicated as follows on charts of sailors venturing into the area: "Eleuthera Point. Light flash every 4.5 seconds. Elevation 61 feet. Visibility 6 miles." The observer is standing at an elevation of about fifty feet. To the leeward, Exuma Sound side of the island is a section of vegetation that is much less dense and thorny than the usual bush. Perhaps because it is exposed, or for other reasons, this area has not been exploited for agriculture. Perhaps this is close to the true natural vegetation of the island. Turning the other way and looking north along the Atlantic shore are miles of seldom visited and unspoiled beach. Looking southeastward, out to sea, the cliffs of the next member of the Bahamian archipelago, Little San Salvador Island, are barely but unmistakably visible across ten miles of water. Looking down into the crystalline water, for which the Bahamas are justly famous, any fish that may be in the vicinity can be easily seen. Here and at other places on Eleuthera it is easy to dream of Robinson Crusoe and the grandeur of the unspoiled island. But the automatic light blinks once every 4.5 seconds and about a mile away people in Bannerman Town are busy at the mundane activities necessary to sustain a human community.

Bannerman Town is situated along a road that roughly parallels the main Eleutheran road. Spurs join it to the main road at two points, one at the southern end of the settlement and the other near the northern end. This parallel road was the main road in the days before tourism. Although impassable in parts by automobile and in other parts now incorporated in the present system of roads, the remnants can still be traced as a

path on topographic maps. Generally close to the leeward shore, it links all the settlements of the island.
In South Eleuthera it runs from Bannerman Town to Weymss
Bight to Deep Creek to Greencastle to Rock Sound, then
on to Tarpum Bay. When this was the only road and the
chief mode of transportation was walking, occasionally
supplemented by horses, this circuitous route of perhaps thirty miles indicates that there was very little
direct communication between Bannerman Town and the
administrative center of Rock Sound. Informants indicate that Bannerman Town was a much larger place during
the pineapple boom. Many ruins of houses interspersed
between present ones attest to this. Although it was
larger in the past, it does not appear to have been an
administrative or trade center. Informants and writings
indicate that pineapples were collected on small boats,
"lighters," at settlements such as Bannerman Town and
carried along the coast for transfer to larger "freight-
ers" at what remain to this day the commercial and governmental centers of the island: Rock Sound and Governor's Harbour.

Realizing that the population is about one tenth
the size of Rock Sound, it is a surprise to learn that
Bannerman Town is approximately the same length, two
miles. Technically, the community is divided into two
settlements, Bannerman Town and Millers. The distinction was probably important in pre-emancipation days
when a family named "Miller" operated an "estate" in the
area, the remains of which can still be seen. Nowadays
the two are functionally one, regarded so by the government and will be so regarded here.

In stark contrast to Rock Sound, this settlement
is lineal and the twenty-five households are scattered
over such a distance that it is seldom that more than
two can be viewed at the same time. The latest houses
to be built are of concrete block, but much smaller than
those of Rock Sound. Differentiating these dwellings
more than size is the fact that there is no public electricity in Bannerman Town and no running water in any
of the houses. Most houses are of wood-frame construction or the earliest type of house found on the island:
wattle-and-daub. The wattle-and-daub houses are usually
square with wooden shutters and a pyramid-shaped "hip"
roof. Elsewhere on the island the roof is invariably
shingled with wood. Only in Bannerman Town do some
people live under thatched roofs.

66

With such a low population density and low degree
of mechanization the vicinity of Bannerman Town is
usually very quiet.   Automobiles and trucks can be heard
approaching from some distance away and people can iden-
tify who is coming from the particular sounds of the
various vehicles. Within the settlement the virtually
exclusive mode of transportation is walking. Shoes are
seldom worn because they are doubly expensive, relative
to the U.S.A. First, the initial price is higher because transportation charges and a ten percent import
duty must be added to the price. Second, shoes wear
out more quickly on the sharp limestone terrain.

Almost all adults, male and female, are farmers.
The farmer is easy to recognize on Eleuthera through the
two invariable tools of the trade: the cutlass and the
carrying bag woven of palmetto fibre. In Latin America
the cutlass would be called a machette, but "cutlass"
is a fitting term because it describes the preferred
size and shape, approximately thirty inches by two inches. This is truly a versatile tool, used for bush
and weed clearing, digging planting holes in the lime-
stone-surrounded pockets of soil, as well as for har-
vesting crops and gathering firewood or fodder.

The bag usually measures about eighteen inches
square. It is made of strips of woven palmetto palm
fibre, three to four inches wide. These strips are
used to make hats as well as bags and are shipped from
Eleuthera and other out-islands to be used as the basic
construction material in Nassau's tourist-oriented
"straw" market. For the bag, the strips are sewn hori-
zontally until the desired height is attained. Narrower strips are used for handles sewn to each side at the
top and to reinforce the seam at one end and at the bot-
tom. Curious neighbors and visiting anthropologists
seldom know exactly what is in one of these bags, but
on the way to the field it will usually contain a bot-
tle of water and something to eat, perhaps some cold
fish from last night's dinner to be warmed over a fire
at midday. On the way home the bag may contain something that has been harvested, but a large or heavy
load will be balanced adroitly on top of the head.

Since the only local wage labor is low-paid work
in the nearby pineapple field and since remoteness
makes it difficult to travel to other settlements for
work, one has a sense in Bannerman Town of being in a
different age: the age before tourism began, but after

MAP 4: BANNERMAN TOWN

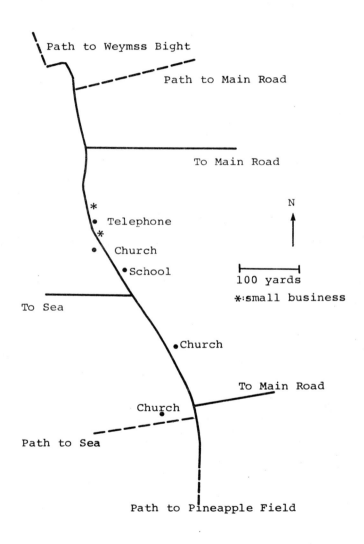

Path to Weymss Bight

Path to Main Road

To Main Road

N

*
• Telephone
*
• Church
• School

├─────────┤
100 yards

*:small business

To Sea

• Church

To Main Road

Church
•

Path to Sea

Path to Pineapple Field

MAP 5: GREENCASTLE

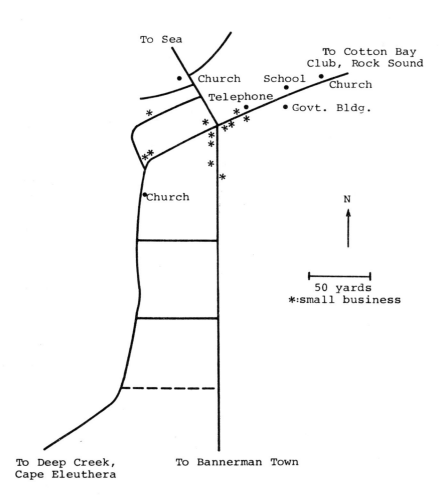

the boom days of pineapple had ended, an age in which
Eleutheran settlements were in the economic basal me-
tabolism of "subsistence-plus" agriculture. As has
been seen, this is the view of the inhabitants. One
woman commented that it must be hard for someone from
the U. S. to spend a summer in the settlement because
"we don't have a jukebox."

With some knowledge of the opposite ends of the
spectrum, it is easy to picture medium-sized Greencastle.
Agriculture is important but a considerable number of
people are able to engage primarily in activities other
than agriculture, the nearby Cotton Bay Club being the
major employer. In physical appearance, Greencastle
resembles the old section of Rock Sound minus the government buildings. Houses are generally of the wood
frame type and clustered, not the dispersed lineal
pattern of Bannerman Town. As in Rock Sound, small
business operations tend to be located randomly amidst
the houses. Electricity and running water are available. A few houses on the periphery are in the U. S.
suburban style, including TV antenna. Cars and trucks
are in frequent evidence, less than Rock Sound, but
much more than Bannerman Town. As in Bannerman Town,
but not Rock Sound, pigs and herds of goats roam freely
in the streets.

This discussion of the present outward appearance
of South Eleuthera has been brief and not intended to
be a thorough description. The intent has been to
demonstrate that the modernizing forces of tourism have
differentially affected the settlements of Eleuthera.
Rock Sound has been affected heavily, Bannerman Town
hardly at all, and Greencastle to a medium degree.
This is obvious to Eleutheran and non-Eleutheran alike.
Not so obvious is the topic of the next chapter: How
have the people been affected?

CHAPTER 8

INWARD APPEARANCES

We may examine economic and social
change in a community as changes in the
real world (the phenomenal world of the
scientist) or as changes in the phenomenal world of its members. Most analy-
ses of change follow one or the other
approach, or mix up the two without
clearly distinguishing between them.
A great deal of what is called "cultural" change in social scientific literature also amounts to no more than change
in a community's real or phenomenal conditions, only incidentally including
changes in the criteria by which people
discern things, their beliefs about
things, their purposes in relation to
them, or their principles for dealing
with them (Goodenough 1966: 257-258).

In the years that saw the advent and development
of tourism on Eleuthera a growing and now immense amount
of effort has been expended in anthropology and social
science generally attempting to understand and thus to
facilitate the process by which marginal peoples, the
"have nots," can become prospering segments of the glo-
bal industrial system. This is the literature of economic development and modernization. In this effort a
number of conceptual tools have risen to prominence in
the social scientific community, then entered a period
of declining usage. Among these might be mentioned
"cultural deprivation," "the image of limited good,"
"the culture of poverty," "achievement motivation."
All have been subjected to severe scholarly attack, but
their lack of widespread acceptance or demise is also
attributable to the fact that they have not proven very
useful in smoothing the path for "emerging" peoples.

Examination of the four concepts mentioned suggests
a common failing of these and others, a failing that
points to a different and perhaps more useful way of
attacking the problem. The common failing is not recog-
nizing that culture can be regarded as having two aspects that are not necessarily in direct linkage. These
aspects are here called "covert" and "overt" culture and
are derived from the thinking of Ward Goodenough, as

71

expressed in the quotation that opens this chapter.

"Cultural deprivation" is a phrase used frequently by U. S. educators in the 1960's. It encapsulates a theory that the reason ghetto peoples of the U. S. are marginal is that they lack experience outside the ghettos, they have not learned how to behave in the society outside the ghetto, i.e. they lack "culture." The remedy, the path of emergence suggested by this theory was to expose ghetto children to the wider society with such projects as "Operation Headstart," in which preschool ghetto children were taken to zoos and in various other ways given more exposure to the wider society. The problem with this approach is that it places all the burden of emergence on the individual ghetto child, ignoring the multitudinous ways the wider society acts to block the emergence of ghetto people. "Culture" is restricted in meaning to something covert, within individual persons, that enables them to function effectively within a society. In a sense very foreign to anthropology, some people have more of it than others.

Anthropologist Oscar Lewis gives a more sophisticated but very controversial view of this same group with his concept, "the culture of poverty" (cf. Leacock 1971 and bibliography). Lewis argues persuasively that far from being deprived of culture, people ghettoized in poverty relative to their mainstream culture anywhere in the world develop a way of life, or culture, adapted to survival in that situation. Lewis considers culture to be both something embedded within the individual and as an external environment to be coped with and adapted to. The problem with this approach is that the interface between the two aspects of culture is not explored. If the internal culture of poverty is linked to the external cultural situation of poverty, how strong is the link? If the overt culture of poverty were changed, i.e. poverty were removed, would the covert, individual culture be serviceable under the new conditions, or would it, indeed could it change too? By failing to answer these questions, failing to examine the relationship between variation in overt culture and variation in covert culture, Lewis gives many readers the impression that the culture of poverty is a vicious circle with no way out.

Social psychologist David McClelland and associates have been the main proponents of the concept "achievement motivation." The crux of his thinking is that marginal peoples can emerge through developing in the individual desire or "need" to achieve. McClelland found that a rise in this need had accompanied the rise of industrialism in Europe (1961). In India he found that a program designed to raise levels of need-achievement actually did promote economic achievement (McClelland and Winter 1971). While more focused than cultural deprivation, the problem with this "Dale Carnegie" approach is the same. It places all the burden on change within the individual. It assumes that all societies have equal opportunity for individual achievement. One suspects that in a society with actual sparce resources, raising the general level of need for achievement might cause more frustration and general unhappiness than economic development or emergence.

Just as it could be said that Oscar Lewis provided an anthropological response to the notion of "cultural deprivation," it could be said that George Foster has responded to "need-achievement" with "the image of limited good" (1965). Foster proposes that peasants everywhere in the world face a situation of sparce resources, particularly the one resource that is most important to a peasant: land. Any land an individual peasant gains is gained at the expense of another individual. From this situation peasants come to view all good things, even friendship, as being in short supply and gained at the expense of others. This is "the image of limited good." Like Oscar Lewis, Foster argues that a covert, internalized culture develops to cope with an external situation. Unlike Lewis, Foster does not present the situation as a vicious circle. His concluding sentence challenges the McClelland approach and suggests a path of emergence for peasants. "Change cognitive orientation through changing access to opportunity, and the peasant will do very well indeed; and his n-Achievement will take care of itself" (1965: 312).

Foster suggests that n-Achievement is but a small, trifling part of "cognitive orientation," or what is here called covert culture. His statement also suggests the nature of the link between covert and overt culture: simply change the overt culture or part of it, "access to opportunity," and the covert will change in accordance. Foster's explicit statement is in direct contradiction to the implicit assumption of the n-Achievement and cultural deprivation schools of thought which suggest changing the covert and assume that changes in the overt will necessarily follow.

73

The contention here is that the theories underlying the four concepts discussed and many other theories of development and modernization have failed to prove useful because they have not seriously investigated the manner in which overt and covert cultural change are linked.

In addition to the two types of linkage just discussed, there has been an allusion to a third possibility: changes in covert culture with no change in overt culture. For example people might become less culturally deprived or raise their level of n-Achievement with no corresponding change in their outward circumstances.

A fourth logical possibility is that there can be change in the overt culture without change in the covert. In other words, outward circumstances could change with people remaining unchanged. This possibility is seldom considered. It would seem that the majority of U. S. social scientists, especially non-anthropologists, feel that people must change before outward circumstances can change. George Foster challenges this view, but feels that people will change as outward circumstances change. Although perhaps difficult to envision, this fourth type of possible linkage might be regarded as the smoothest and least disruptive way in which marginal peoples can emerge into the world industrial system. If basic beliefs, values, attitudes and other components of the covert culture of individuals can remain unchanged as outward circumstances change, the implication would be that their covert culture is adapted to a wide variety of overt cultures. Such linkage would seem desirable even in developed nations, which now seem to be changing rapidly. It would be an antidote to future shock. This is the type of linkage that anthropologists proudly claim to possess themselves, enabling them to tolerate and come to intellectual terms with overt cultural environments considerably different from their accustomed ones.

As was indicated in the last chapter, there is considerable variation in the overt cultures of the settlements of Eleuthera. Bannerman Town, Greencastle, and Rock Sound are located at quite different positions of emergence into the world industrial system, with isolated, subsistence-farming oriented Bannerman Town the least emerged, or most "traditional" and Rock Sound, with its considerable exposure to the outside world and opportunity for wage labor, the most emerged, or most "modern." This chapter presents and discusses the results of two measurements of the covert culture, values and attitudes, in each of the settlements. It attempts to examine the linkage between changes in overt culture and changes in covert culture on this island.

In 1970 indigenous Bahamian values were measured. The means of measurement was developed by William B. Rodgers in his study of the Bahamian out-island of Abaco (Rodgers and Gardner 1969). Rodgers compiled a list of the ten adjectives Abaconians used most frequently to label positive traits in one another. The ten terms are presented in Table 7-1 below. Pairing these indigenous "values" with each other in all possible ways, a list of forty-five pairs is generated. To determine how the values are ranked in a particular settlement, subjects are asked which of each pair is more important, e.g. "Which is it better to be: 'generous' or 'successful'?" By totaling the number of times a term is chosen over other terms, a ranking of the ten values for the settlement can be established.

The terms Rodgers used are also in frequent use on Eleuthera. His "values test" was administered to a sample of twenty persons in each of the three settlements. In Bannerman Town an adult from each available household was tested. In Greencastle and Rock Sound, subjects were randomly chosen from lists of households. The results of this test are presented in Table 7-1.

TABLE 7-1: RESULT OF RODGERS VALUES TEST

	Rank			Change in Rank	
	BT	GC	RS	BT to GC	BT to RS
Christian	1	1	1	0	0
Mind-own-business	2	10	3	-8	-1
Honest	3	2	2	1	1
Sober	4	7	4	-3	0
Friendly	5	9	9	-4	-4
Mannerly	6.5	3	6	3.5	0.5
Responsible	6.5	4.5	5	2	1.5
Generous	8	5	10	3	-2
Successful	9	4.5	7.5	4.5	1.5
Agreeable	10	8	7.5	2	2.5

BT: Bannerman Town; GC: Greencastle; RS: Rock Sound

The results indicate that Rock Sound is considerably closer to Bannerman Town in ranking of values than is Greencastle. Seven of the ten have changed less than two ranks between Bannerman Town and Rock Sound, while eight have changed two ranks or more between Bannerman Town and Greencastle. On the average values have changed 1.24 ranks in Rock Sound, but 3.10 in Greencastle. Further, the changes are not consistently in one direction. Only the value placed on being "agreeable" changes consistently as the settlements changed in outward appearance along the scale of modernity. Although this test gives merely one glimpse at inward appearances, the results suggest the possibility that on Eleuthera, changes in covert culture do not correspond in a direct lineal way with changes in overt culture.

The findings from the values test are supported by the results of a second measure of covert culture taken in 1972. Approximately the same sample was administered the Kahl test of individual modernism (Kahl 1968). A major difference between this and the values test is that here the items are derived not from within the culture of the Bahamas, but from social-scientific theories about how people in modern circumstances are different from those in traditional circumstances. Since there are serious questions about the validity of current measures of individual modernism (cf. Swanson 1975, Armer and Schnaiberg 1972 and bibliography), the intent of administering the test on Eleuthera was not to achieve precise measurement of individuals or settlements on covert modernism, but merely to see whether the pattern of changes in responses corresponded or did not correspond with the apparent changes in overt modernity of the settlements.

In the Kahl test, 58 questions tap fourteen computer-derived "factors" of individual modernism. The factors and the collective responses of each settlement to each question are available from the author. The purpose of this chapter is served by a summary of the results. Of the fourteen factors, only the last and weakest shows a consistent progression of individual modernism linked to overt modernism in the three settlements. In all the others, Greencastle appears to be either the most traditional or the most modern. In the 58 questions Greencastle gives a more traditional response than the other two settlements on 27 (47%). It gives the most modern response on 10 (17%). The Kahl test gives a second indication that the people of Greencastle are more different from the people of Bannerman Town than are the people of Rock Island.

The findings of the two "objective" measures are substantiated by more impressionistic but equally important, "common sense" evidence. It was indicated earlier that the people of Rock Sound tend to stereotype the people of Greencastle as "quarrelsome," a negative evaluation, but regard the people of Bannerman Town as "honest and hard-working," a positive evaluation. Court statistics support the stereotype of Greencastle. Here also it is not midway between Bannerman Town and Rock Sound, but produces more court cases and police action than any other settlement of South Eleuthera. According to a survey taken as part of this project, Greencastle shows the highest level of church attendance of the three settlements, many people attending nightly. Dances occur more frequently in Greencastle than in the other two. Greencastle is the only settlement in the district where a local business establishment, "The Continental Club," was observed to advertise over the Bahamas radio station, Nassau-based ZNS. In contrast to the other settlements, the people of Greencastle place low value on "minding one's own business." To set the "quarrelsome" stereotype in a broader framework, Greencastle seems to be a place in ferment. In South Eleuthera it seems to be the lively place, the place "where the action is."

The priori assumption in many social scientific quarters that change in overt culture is linked in a direct, lineal way to changes within individuals, with one or the other type of change casual, seems refuted by a variety of evidence from Eleuthera. Here the end points of a continuum of outward change appear to be associated with little change in individuals. On Eleuthera it seems to be at the midpoint of outward change that the changes in individuals have occurred. Why this is the case can be answered with reasonable certainty only by further research, but some suggestions can be offered.

As to why Greencastle appears to be a community in ferment, there is a widespread anthropological principle that a little change is a dangerous thing, especially if the systemic ramifications of a change in part of the system are not anticipated before the change is introduced. Most anthropologists possess a stock of anecdotes illustrating how a seemingly small change can have widespread, usually detrimental, consequences. A classic case is Lauriston Sharp's "Steel Axes for Stone Age Australians" (1953) in which a social system was thrown

into turmoil by the well-intentioned giving away of
steel axes. In "New Lives for Old," Margaret Mead
documents a case of successful cultural change through
changing the entire system all at once, not just a few
isolated parts. She concludes: "It is easier to shift
from being a South Sea Islander to being a New Yorker
. . . than to shift from being a perfectly adjusted
traditional South Sea Islander to a partly civilized,
partly acculturated South Sea Islander" (1956: 376).

Greencastle is a case where there has been a small
change, an increase in opportunity for wage labor,
giving it clearly more than its neighbor Bannerman Town,
but clearly less than its other neighbor, Rock Sound.
It would seem reasonable to suggest that this has caused
frustrations in the populace, upsetting the otherwise
fairly stable covert culture of the island as people
strike out in new directions to achieve their aspira-
tions.

More important to the goal of better comprehending
the dynamics of the process by which marginal peoples
emerge is the question, why do Eleutherans appear to
exhibit basically "type four linkage" between overt and
covert culture: considerable change in outward circumstances with little difference between traditional and
modern settlements in the values and attitudes held by
individuals? An answer to this question requires a
return to the theme of this work, Eleuthera as an exposed island. The history of the island and the colony
is one of cyclical boom and bust controlled by forces in
the wider world. It is an anthropoligical maxim that
every culture is an adaptation to its environment.
Eleutherans and Bahamians have had to adapt to an environment of fluctuating economic prosperity and fluctuating reliance on the outside world. It would seem to
be a reasonable proposition that these people developed
the covert side of their culture to cope with either
extreme. Since the historical ups and downs have been
rapid, the case of Greencastle may indicate that an
adaptation yet to be made, and perhaps difficult everywhere, is to be caught in the middle, neither up (outwardly modern) nor down (outwardly traditional). The
problems of partial change are well documented. The
important lesson of the Eleutheran experience for social
science is that some groups of people may have covert
cultures adapted to a wide variety of outward circumstances.

CHAPTER 9

THE REAL TROPICAL ISLAND

You're from Minnesota? That's nice
country around there. I worked for the
Green Giant Company at LeSeur (Subsistence farmer in Greencastle).

This work could be regarded as a dissertation on
the meaning of the word, "island." For reasons which
should now seem fanciful, at least with regard to the
island examined, Roget lists the word with "oasis" as
synonyms of "isolated." Roget is not giving a strictly
personal connotation of the word, but expresses a meaning that seems widespread in Western culture from ancient Greek times.

This work has proceeded on the premise that a
generalization useful to understanding the island of
Eleuthera and its context, the Bahama Islands, can be
achieved by inverting the popular conception and regarding the island as the opposite of an oasis and the
opposite of isolated.

Consideration of the natural ecology of islands
indicates that they are incapable of supporting human
life in their pristine state. As with a spaceship,
people must supply them. This unoasis-like quality of
islands is particularly evident in the small, low,
limestone-clad Bahamas. Aboriginal population density
was very low. The Spaniards ignored them except to
capture slaves and colonized mainly the largest and
least island-like entities in the Caribbean: Cuba,
Hispaniola, Puerto Rico.

The English appear to have been more driven to the
Bahamas by political forces than drawn to them by their
resources. With the advent of this European colonization any notion of the Bahamas as isolated or independent from the rest of the world must be abandoned.
Considerable linkage is implied by the very word "colony," but some colonies are more strongly linked to and
dependent on the outer world than others because they
are less naturally endowed, less self-sufficient, less
oasis-like. The history of the Bahamas is characterized
by continuous and varying efforts to exploit and profit
from fluctuating outside world conditions.

Data from the latest census indicate that the net
profits for the average citizen, though considerably
greater than in many developing countries including
Caribbean neighbors, are not very great relative to its
large, prosperous, and constantly visiting and intruding
neighbor, the U.S.A. As the U.S.A. is called "a nation
of immigrants," it is understandable that the tiny island
nation might be called "a nation of emigrants."

But many Eleutherans and Bahamians choose to remain in the islands. They presumably stay because they
participate in a social and cultural system that works,
and because they perceive the known benefits of staying
as outweighing the less certain benefits of leaving.
The social system has here been characterized as "fragmented," but it is fragmented in an island way that
could be given the more positive label "rugged individualism." It is not the physically numbing type of fragmentation found in urban-industrial societies that is
associated with ultra-specialization of jobs, such as
assembly-line work, not the type recognized by Edward
Sapir in his 1924 distinction of "Culture: Genuine and
Spurious."

The fragmentation on Eleuthera appears to result
from occupational multiplicity. Occupational multiplicity provides in the present the thing for which the
island was originally named: freedom. Frequently
evident in conversation and also indicated by the ranking of values presented in the last chapter, Eleutherans
generally subordinate financial success and interper-
sonal solidarity to values associated with personal
autonomy. Fully aware that it is not an oasis, many
Eleutherans see good reasons to remain in their unisolated island home.

Perhaps the most important result of considering
Eleuthera as exposed rather than an isolated oasis is
the conclusion in the preceding chapter that to adapt
to this situation Eleutherans and Bahamians have developed a covert culture, a cognitive orientation, that
can remain unchanged in a wide variety of outward circumstances, be they labeled "traditional" versus "modern" or in other ways. Ward Goodenough feels that many
people may be like Eleutherans in this respect:

A great deal of what is called
"cultural" change in social scientific literature amounts to no more

than a change in community's real or
phenomenal conditions, only incidentally including changes in the criteria by which people discern things,
their beliefs about things, their
purposes in relation to them, or
their principles for dealing with them
(1966: 258).

More study of the linkage between covert and overt
culture is indicated. Better understanding of the
linkage might greatly increase the efficiency of efforts
to promote the well-being of developing peoples. As for
the future of the people of Eleuthera and the Bahamas,
George Foster can be paraphrased: Change access to
opportunity and these people will be found looking for
the change and ready to take advantage of it. Relative
to the urban-industrial situation the Bahamas are places
of freedom, tranquility and beauty. With outside resources and attention to the systemic ramifications of
alterations, Eleuthera and the Bahamas can add prosperity and greater well-being to their beauty.

REFERENCES

Abrahams, Roger D.
  1964 Deep Down in the Jungle, Hatboro PA:
       Folklore Associates.

Armer, M. and A. Schnaiberg
  1972 Measuring Individual Modernity: A Near Myth.
       American Sociological Review 37: 301-316.

Belin, J. N.
  1758 Description Geographiques des Iles Antilles
       possedess par les Anglois. Paris.

Bruce, Peter Henry
  1782 Bahamian Interlude. Edited by Richard Kent.
       Republished London 1949: J. Culmer.

Carneiro, Robert L.
  1960 Slash-and-Burn Agriculture: A Closer Look at
       its Implications for Settlement Patterns. In
       Anthony F. Wallace (ed.) Men and Cultures.
       Philadelphia: University of Pennsylvania
       Press.

Comitas, Lambros
  1973 Occupational Multiplicity in Rural Jamaica.
       In Lambros Comitas and David Lowenthal (eds.)
       Work and Family Life: West Indian Perspec-
       tives. Garden City, NY: Doubleday, 157-174.

Craton, Michael
  1968 A History of the Bahamas. (2nd Edition)
       London: Collins.

Cruxent, Jose M. and Irving Rouse
  1969 Early Man in the West Indies. Scientific
       American 221: 42-52.

Darwin, Charles
  1859 The Origin of Species by Means of Natural
       Selection. London. Reprinted n.d. New York:
       Random House.

Dillard, J. L.
  1972 Black English: Its History and Usage in the
       United States. New York: Random House.

Domingo, W. A.
1956 British West Indian Federation - - A Critique.
Kingston, Jamaica: The Gleaner Co. Ltd.

Depuch, Etienne
1974 Bahamas Handbook and Businessman's Annual:
1964-1975 Nassau: Etienne Depuch, Jr.
Publications.

Foster, George M.
1965 Peasant Society and the Image of Limited Good.
American Anthropologist 67: 293-315.

Gonzales, Nancie L. Solien
1969 Black Carib Household Structure: A Study of
Migration and Modernization. Seattle: University of Washington Press.

Goodenough, Ward
1966 Cooperation in Change: An Anthropological
Approach to Community Development. New York:
Wiley Science Editions.

Granberry, Julian
1955 A Survey of Bahamian Archaeology. Master's
Thesis. Department of Sociology and Anthropology. Granville: University of Florida.
1973 The Lucayans. In S. P. Dupuch (ed.) Bahamas
Handbook and Businessman's Annual. Nassau
Etienne Dupuch, Jr. Publications.

Greenfield, Sidney M.
1966 English Rustics in Black Skin: A Study of
Modern Family Forms in a Pre-industrial Society. New Haven, CT: College and University
Press.

Hannau, Hans W.
1970 The Bahama Islands. Miami: Argos Inc.

Harris, David R.
1965 Plants, Animals, and Man in the Outer Leeward
Islands, West Indies. Berkeley: University
of California Press.

Herskovits, Melville J.
1941 The Myth of the Negro Past. Boston: Beacon
Press.

84

Higgs, Mrs. Leslie
1969 Bush Medicine in the Bahamas. Nassau:
Private Publication.

Hoffman, Charles A., Jr.
1967 Bahama Prehistory: Cultural Adaptation to an
Island Environment. Ph.D. Dissertation.
Tucson University of Arizona.
1970 The Palmetto Grove Site on San Salvador,
Bahamas. Contributions of the Florida State
Museum, Social Sciences, No. 16. Gainesville:
University of Florida.

Johnson, Doris L.
1972 The Quiet Revolution in the Bahamas. Nassau:
Family Islands Press.

Kahl, Joseph A.
1968 The Measurement of Modernism: A Study of
Values in Brazil and Mexico. Austin: The
University of Texas Press.

Kimball, Solon T.
1975 Review of "The Coming of Post-Industrial Society" by Daniel Bell. American Anthropologist
77: 365-366.

Kiste, Robert C.
1974 The Bikinians: A Study in Forced Migration.
Menlo Park, CA: Cummings Publishing Company.

Kochman, Thomas
1969 "Rapping" in the Black Ghetto." Transaction,
February 1969: 26-34.

Las Casas, Bartolome de
1560 History of the Indies. Andree Collard (trans.
and ed.) 1971. New York: Harper and Row.

Lefroy, Sir. J. H.
1879 Memorials of Bermuda (2 vols. 1515-1685).
London.

Leacock, Eleanor Burke (ed.)
1971 The Culture of Poverty: A Critique. New York:
Simon and Schuster.

McClelland, David C.
1961 The Achieving Society. Princeton, NJ: Van
Nostrand.

McClelland, David C. and David G. Winter
    1971 Motivating Economic Achievement. New York:
        Free Press.

McKinnen, D.
    1804 A Tour through the British West Indies in the
        Years 1802 and 1803. London.

Mead, Margaret
    1956 New Lives for Old: Cultural Transformation--
        Manus 1928-1953. New York: William Morrow
        and Co.

Mooney, Charles N.
    1905 Soils of the Bahama Islands. In George Bur-
        bank Shattuck (ed.) The Bahama Islands. New
        York: Macmillan. 147-184.

Otterbein, Keith F.
    1966 The Andros Islanders. Laurence, KS: Univer-
        sity of Kansas Press.

Padilla, Elena
    1960 Contemporary Social-Rural Types in the Carib-
        bean Region. In Vera Rubin (ed.) Caribbean
        Studies: A Symposium.

Pindling, L. O.
    1927 Independence for the Commonwealth of the
        Bahamas. (Green Paper) Nassau: Bahamas
        Government.

Riley, Joseph H.
    1905 Birds of the Bahama Islands. In George Bur-
        bank Shattuck (ed.) The Bahama Islands. New
        York: Macmillan 347-370.

Rodgers, William B.
    1965 The Wages of Change: An Anthropological Study
        of the Effects of Economic Development on Some
        Negro Communities in the Out-Island Bahamas.
        Ph.D. Dissertation. Stanford University.

Rodgers, William B. and Richard E. Gardner
    1969 Linked Changes in Values and Behavior in the
        Out-Island Bahamas. American Anthropologist
        71: 21-35.

Rouse, Irving
1964 Prehistory of the West Indies. Science 144:
     499-513.
1966 Mesoamerica and the Eastern Caribbean Area.
     In Robert Washope (ed.) Handbook of Middle
     American Indians. Austin: University of
     Texas Press.

Sapir, Edward
1924 Culture, Genuine and Spurious. American
     Journal of Sociology 29: 401-429.

Sauer, Carl Ortwin
1966 The Early Spanish Main, Berkeley: University
     of California Press.

Sharer, Cyrus J.
1955 The Population Growth of the Bahama Islands.
     Ph.D. Dissertation. University of Michigan.

Sharp, Lauriston
1953 Steel Axes for Stone-Age Australians. Human
     Organization 11: 17-22.

Smith, Bernard
1960 Europeans' Vision and the South Pacific 1768-
     1850: A Study in the History of Art and Ideas.
     New York: Oxford University Press.

Springer, High W.
1967 Federation in the Caribbean: An Attempt that
     Failed. International Organization 21: 758-
     775.

Steward, Julian H. et al
1956 The People of Puerto Rico. Urbana: Univer-
     sity of Illinois Press.

Swanson, Guy E.
1975 Review of Becoming Modern: Individual Change
     in Six Developing Countries by Alex Inkeles
     and David H. Smith. Science 188: 829-831.

Tertullien, J. Egbert
1971 Statistical Abstract 1970. Nassau: Bahamas
     Government Department of Statistics.
1972 Commonwealth of the Bahama Islands: Report of
     the 1970 Census of Population. Nassau:
     Bahamas Government Department of Statistics.

Tidrick, Gene
    1966 Some Aspects of Jamaican Emigration to the
        United Kingdom 1953-1962. Social and Economic
        Studies 15: 22-39.

U. S. Bureau of the Census
    1974 The Social and Economic Status of the Black
        Population of the United States, 1973.
        Washington, D. C.: Government Printing
        Office.

Wagely, Charles
    1960 Plantation America: A Culture Sphere. In
        Vera Rubin (ed.) Caribbean Studies: A Sympo-
        sium. Seattle: University of Washington
        Press. 3-13.

Wallace, Susan J.
    1970 Bahamian Scene, Philadelphia: Dorrance and
        Company.

Whitten, Norman and John F. Szwed
    1970 Afro-American Anthropology. New York: Free
        Press.

Wilkinson, Henry C.
    1933 The Adventurers of Bermuda. London: Oxford
        University Press.

Williams, Eric
    1970 From Columbus to Castro: The History of the
        Caribbean 1492-1969. London: Andre Deutsch.

Wolper, Ruth G. Durlacher
    1964 A New Theory Identifying the Locale of Colum-
        bus's Light, Landfall, and Landing. Smithso-
        nian Miscellaneous Collections.

Wylly, William
    1789 A Short Account of the Bahama Islands. London.

Young, Everild
    1966 Eleuthera: The Island Called Freedom. London:
        Regency Press.

Zimmerman, Elwood C.
    1963 Nature of the Land Biota. In F. R. Fosberg
        (ed.) Man's Place in the Island Ecosystem: A
        Symposium. Honolulu: Bishop Museum Press.
        57-63.

88